P9-AQX-436

The Hyperactive Child & the Learning Disabled Child

Also by Paul H. Wender

Minimal Brain Dysfunction in Children

The Hyperactive Child & the Learning Disabled Child

A HANDBOOK FOR PARENTS

New, Revised, and Enlarged Edition of *The Hyperactive Child*

PAUL H. WENDER, M.D.
and ESTHER H. WENDER, M.D.

CROWN PUBLISHERS, INC., NEW YORK

© 1978 by Paul H. Wender and Esther H. Wender
All rights reserved. No part of this book may be reproduced or utilized
in any form or by any means, electronic or mechanical, including
photocopying, recording, or by any information storage and retrieval
system, without permission in writing from the publisher.
Inquiries should be addressed to Crown Publishers, Inc., One Park Avenue,
New York, N.Y. 10016
Printed in the United States of America
Published simultaneously in Canada by
General Publishing Company Limited

LIBRARY OF CONGRESS CATALOGING IN PUBLICATION DATA

Wender, Paul H   1934-
    The hyperactive child and the learning disabled child.

    Published in 1973 under title: The hyperactive child.
    Includes index.
    1. Hyperactive children.   I.   Wender, Esther H., joint author.   II.   Title.
RJ506.H9W45   1978   618.9′28′58   78-19018
ISBN 0-517-53473-8

Contents

Preface

In 1973 the first version of this book appeared, *The Hyperactive Child* by Paul H. Wender. During several years of treating hyperactive children, we had discovered that the parents of such children needed information about the nature, causes, and treatment of hyperactivity, and that there was no book available presenting such data in a form suitable for the concerned layperson. *The Hyperactive Child* was written in response to the need for such a book, drawing on clinical and research experience as previously summarized in a book for physicians and other professionals working with children (P. H. Wender, *Minimal Brain Dysfunction in Children*. New York: Wiley, 1971).

Since *The Hyperactive Child* was written, child psychiatrists have learned more about hyperactivity. One important aspect of what has been learned is that learning disabilities frequently accompany hyperactivity. Therefore, considerable material on learning disabilities has been added to the present version of the book. We wish to emphasize that this does not mean that the two disorders always occur together. Thus, for some parents the entire book will be relevant, but for other parents only the parts on hyperactivity will be pertinent, and for still others, only the parts on learning disabilities will be important.

In addition to what has been learned about the relationship between hyperactivity and learning disabilities, much has been learned about new contributions to the medical and psychological management of hyperactivity. Although the original book was authored by one of us (PHW), most of the information presented here on learning disabilities and on new psychological techniques for managing hyperactivity has been provided by the other (EHW); this information has come from her ten years of specialized pediatric practice in the treatment of hyperactive children and learning disabled children. Thus, this updated and expanded book is the product of our joint efforts.

We both dedicate the book to hyperactive children and learning disabled children and their families, in the hope that better understanding will lead to better treatment of these common and frequently misunderstood disorders of childhood.

PAUL H. WENDER, M.D.
ESTHER H. WENDER, M.D.
Salt Lake City, Utah

1

Introduction

There are probably five million hyperactive children in the United States. Hyperactivity is the single most common behavioral disorder seen by child psychiatrists. Although hyperactivity was described by physicians many years ago, only recently has its frequency been recognized. Exact figures are not available, but it seems likely that as many as 5 percent of school-age children have hyperactive problems, frequently accompanied by learning disabilities. Although both hyperactivity and learning disabilities are much more common in boys, they can occur in girls as well.

Along with increasing awareness of the problem of hyperactivity, a better understanding of its causes and treatment has developed. The purpose of this book is to explain to parents the present understanding of this problem and the best techniques for its management. The book should of course be an aid and not a substitute for diagnosis and treatment by qualified physicians. It is designed to answer many of the questions most frequently asked and to describe some of the simple procedures that many parents have found helpful in dealing with their hyperactive children.

Although the problems associated with learning disabilities and the behavioral problems that make up hyperactivity are usually

1

thought of as two different entities, more often than not they occur together in the same child. It is useful to continue to think of the disorders separately, however, for several reasons. First, not all hyperactive children have the kinds of perceptual and thought difficulties that are seen in learning disabilities, and not all children with those kinds of learning disabilities have the behavioral difficulties of the hyperactive child. Second, the treatment of the behavior problems of hyperactivity and the treatment of the academic problems associated with learning disabilities are different. For the most part, therefore, we will discuss them separately.

Hyperactive children are known by many different diagnostic names. Most of these emphasize either different aspects of the children's behavior or different theories of the origin of hyperactivity. Some synonyms for hyperactivity are "maturational lag"; "hyperkinetic reaction"; "immaturity of the nervous system"; and "perceptual-motor problems." Two names for hyperactivity that are often misunderstood by parents are "minimal brain dysfunction" and "minimal cerebral dysfunction." We hope that their meaning will become clearer in the course of our discussion. Finally, two fairly common names are usually incorrect: "minimal brain damage" and "minimal brain injury." Although we shall discuss the causes of hyperactivity later, we wish to emphasize now that most children with hyperactivity are *not* brain-damaged.

The terms *hyperactive* and *hyperactivity* refer to all these conditions; since they will be used innumerable times, the abbreviation HA will stand for both.

This book attempts to summarize what we have observed and learned in treating hundreds of hyperactive children and learning disabled children over a period of more than ten years. In addition, it includes information obtained from the medical literature—a summary of the experiences and findings of other physicians.

In covering the subjects of hyperactivity and learning disabilities, we will use the following words many times: "few," "some," "frequently," "many," "most." In medicine and education one can rarely use such words as "always," "every," or "never." The variety in people is stimulating in everyday life but complicating in medicine. We would like to be able to use the words "always" or "never," but we seldom can. This may make approaching the subject more difficult, but it will present a more realistic picture.

The Characteristics of Hyperactive Children

The task of describing the characteristics of hyperactive children is in some ways a difficult one—not because the attributes are unusual, but because many of the symptoms are present in all children to some degree at some particular time. The parents reading this chapter are apt to conclude that all their children are hyperactive. Before beginning, therefore, let us emphasize that the characteristics listed are not abnormal in themselves; they are only abnormal when they are excessive in degree. What characterizes HA children is the *intensity*, the *persistence*, and the *patterning* of these symptoms.

This chapter should not, of course, be used for diagnosis. Only a clinician who has evaluated many children can accurately decide if a given child is hyperactive. The parent who tries to make the diagnosis alone is like the medical student who, after reading the symptoms of diseases in his text, thinks he has contracted smallpox, leprosy, and cancer within the space of a few weeks. (Fortunately, he recovers just as rapidly.) Parents who suspect that their restless, poorly coordinated, distractible, and demanding child may be hyperactive should seek the service of a competent specialist for diagnosis and a determination as to whether treatment is indeed indicated.

Finally, we wish also to emphasize that since the list of characteristics presented here is an exhaustive one, it does include some traits that are not necessarily present in all hyperactive children.

Hyperactivity

The most common abnormality is, as the name suggests, hyperactivity. Many of these children have been excessively active since early infancy. Parents often report that the child was "different" from the beginning of his life. Frequently, such infants are restless and have feeding problems and colic (intermittent and unexplained crying). They also often have sleeping problems of various sorts: some children fall asleep late and with difficulty, awaken frequently, and arise early; others fall asleep profoundly and are hard to arouse.

As these infants become toddlers, many of them are bundles of energy. The parents frequently report that after an active and restless infancy, the child stood and walked at an early age, and then, like an infant King Kong, burst the bars of his crib and marched forth to destroy the house. He was always on the go, always into everything, always touching (and hence, usually by mistake, breaking) every object in sight. When unwatched for a moment he somehow got to the top of the refrigerator or appeared in the middle of the street. In a twinkling, pots and pans were whisked from cupboards, ashtrays knocked off tables, and lamps overturned. The mother usually felt—and with good cause—that to take her eyes off him for one moment was to invite disaster: the moment her back was turned, something was broken or the toddler's life was in danger.

As the HA child grows older the description changes: he is incessantly in motion, driven like a motor, constantly fidgeting, drumming his fingers, shuffling his feet. He does not stay at any activity long. He pulls all his toys off the shelf, plays with each for a moment and discards it. He cannot color for long. He cannot be read to without quickly losing interest. Of course he is unable to keep from squirming at the dinner table; he may not even be able to sit still in front of the TV set. In the car he drives the other passengers wild. He opens and closes ashtrays, plays with the windows, tugs others' seat belts, and kicks the passengers in the front seat. At school his teacher relates that the child is fidgety, disruptive, unable to sit still in his seat; that he gets up and walks around the classroom, talks out, clowns; and that he jostles, bothers, and annoys his fellow pupils. Sometimes the HA child is as overtalkative as he is overactive, talking as ceaselessly as he moves.

It is important to emphasize that what is different about the HA child is not his level of activity while at play. All children make all adults look like sloths. The HA child cannot be distinguished on the playground. His top speed is not greater than that of other children. What is so different about the HA child is that when he is requested to turn off his motor, he cannot do so for very long. Unlike other children, he cannot inhibit his activity in the home or the classroom. However, it should also be emphasized that the HA child need not *always be* moving. Sometimes he can sit relatively still. For whatever reason, this is most apt to occur when he is getting individual attention from an adult. This is worth remembering because sometimes people who examine the child are misled when he sits more or less still for 10 to 15 minutes. They usually discover their error when they try to increase that time to an hour or so.

There are two additional points to be made about hyperactivity: the first is that *not all HA children are overactive!* There are a few children who have many of the problems that will be discussed later but are not overactive at all, and there are even a few who are less than normally active. Obviously, "hyperactivity" is not a very accurate name for a normally active or sluggish child. Nevertheless, the name "hyperactivity" has stuck, and so *it is important to emphasize that all the other problems can exist without hyperactivity itself.*

The second point is that the hyperactivity is often the first symptom to disappear as the child grows older. Often the other problems persist. Therefore, the fact that a child once was overactive but no longer is does not mean that all the problems are resolved. Many of the other problems may persist and require treatment even though the hyperactivity itself is gone.

Attention Difficulties and Distractibility

Another characteristic of the HA child that is almost always present is easy distractibility or shortness of attention span. This difficulty is not as obvious as the hyperactivity but is of greater practical importance. The HA child lacks stick-to-itiveness.

Young children, in comparison to adults, are relatively lacking in the ability to concentrate and follow through on long and tedious tasks. The HA child acts like a child younger than himself. He is the opposite of the child who sits patiently in the corner painstakingly solving a puzzle and tolerating no interruptions. As a toddler and nursery school student, the HA child rushes quickly from activity to activity, and then seems at a loss for things to do. In school his teacher reports: "You can't get him to pay attention for long. . . . He doesn't finish his work. . . . He doesn't remember what you tell him." At home his mother notices that "he doesn't listen for long . . . he doesn't mind . . . he doesn't remember." The parents must hover over the child in order to get him to do what they want. Told once to eat with his fork and not his hands, he complies, but a few seconds later he is eating with his hands again. He may begin his homework as requested but fail to complete it unless the parents nag him. The child may not necessarily disobey instructions, but in the middle of an assigned job he starts doing something else. Tasks begun are half done. His room is half restored to order; the lawn is half mowed. Sometimes, as will be discussed later, the child appears to remember but is reluctant to comply. Other times he appears to be distracted from the task at hand and forgets.

It is important to note that, like hyperactivity, distractibility need not be present at all times. Often when the child receives individual attention he can attend well for a while. The teacher may report that he "does well with one-to-one attention." A psychologist may report that the child can attend during testing. A pediatrician may report that the child was not inattentive during the brief office examination. They are all correct, but what is important is not how the child can pay attention when an adult is exerting the maximum effort to get him to do so. The question is how well he can persevere in a task on his own, and in this most HA children have considerable difficulty.

In *some* HA children, the distractibility may be concealed by the ability to stick with a particular activity for an unusually long period of time. Usually it is an activity they choose themselves. Sometimes it is a socially useful one (e.g., reading), and sometimes it is not. The child may seem to "lock on" and be undetachable or unusually persistent. The activity may be repeated in a stereotyped and perseverative manner. Such paradoxical behavior in an ostensibly distractible child may confuse a parent, who will ask, "How can he be distractible when he plays with his rock collection for hours on end?" The highly unsatisfactory answer must be: "We do not know, but this is indeed the case."

Attention-Demanding Behavior

In order to develop normally, all children require adult interest, involvement, and attention. As they grow older, they require less but still need the awareness and interest of those whom they love and respect.

The HA child demands attention but this in itself is not what makes him different. He is different and difficult because of his insatiability. Like a younger child he wants to be always on center stage. He may whine, badger, tease, and annoy without stop. The manifestations change with age. As a toddler he may repeat annoying and prohibited activity; as an older child he may attempt to monopolize the dinner-table conversation, clown in the classroom, and show off with his friends at the risk of his neck and to the distress of the law enforcement agencies.

These aspects of his behavior may be concealed by the fact that he sometimes does not manifest certain kinds of affectionate behavior. Many, although far from all, HA children have been undemonstrative. In infancy they were noncuddlers. They did not go to sleep on laps but wiggled off to go about their own business. They were not upset when their mothers left them with baby-sitters or at nursery school. Nonetheless, the same children sometimes figuratively managed to stand at arm's length and prod their parents with a pole.

The demand for attention can be distressing, confusing, and irritating to parents. Since the child demands so much they feel they have not given him what he needs. Since they cannot understand how to satisfy him, they feel deficient. Finally, because the child may cling and poke simultaneously and endlessly, they feel angry.

Impulsivity

A very frequently described characteristic of HA children is "impulsivity" or "poor impulse control." Every young child wants what he wants when he wants it. He acts without reflection or consideration of the consequences. The ability to tolerate delays, to count to ten, to think before acting, tends to develop with age. Again, the HA child behaves like a child several years younger than his chronological age.

He rapidly becomes upset when things or people fail to behave as he would have them behave. Toys get kicked (and sometimes broken), brothers and sisters and classmates are apt to get socked when they don't do what *they* should.

He acts on the spur of the moment. He rushes into the street, onto the ledge, up the tree. As a result he receives more than his share of cuts, bruises, abrasions, and trips to the doctor. He wears out clothes or destroys toys—not maliciously but unthinkingly. It seemed like fun to walk in the street in his Sunday best; he wondered what would happen if he pulled that knob on the toy.

Impulsivity is also shown in poor planning and judgment. It is difficult to specify how much planning and judgment one should expect of children, but, again, HA children show less of these qualities than seems to be age-appropriate. They are more likely than most children to run off in several directions at once. They are disorderly and disorganized. Their impulsivity combines with their distractibility to produce untidy rooms, sloppy dress (untucked shirts, unzippered zippers), unfinished assignments, careless reading and writing.

Another area that is a problem in some HA children is bladder and bowel control, and it may be related to their impulsivity. When younger, some HA children may wet or soil themselves slightly during the day. They seem to pay no attention to their "pressing needs" and overflow somewhat. Bed-wetting, which occurs in about 10 percent of all six-year-old boys, seems to be more common in HA children. It may be that bed-wetting in some HA children is related to unusually deep sleep, but this is not certain. The relationship between HA and bed-wetting is important to recognize because "accidents" and bed-wetting are sometimes assumed to be a sign of anatomical abnormalities or deep psychological problems. Often, however, they are instead a manifestation of hyperactivity and respond to the general treatment prescribed for hyperactivity.

Social impulsivity—antisocial behavior—is *sometimes* a problem in HA children. At some time all children steal, all children lie, most children play with matches. As they grow older most children learn to inhibit these impulses. A few HA children do not; they take, lie, or light matches whenever they want to. Now the HA itself does not explain *why* children wish to do these things. Children steal for a wide variety of reasons. Stealing may result from a simple desire to have or from a desire to have things that would buy affection; it may be an attempt to achieve status in a group; it may be a source of excitement; or it may be a means of retaliating, or obtaining attention or punishment. What is important is that if these motives occur in the HA child, he is less able than other children to control himself. It should be obvious that treatment of such a child would require a twofold approach: dealing with the specific motivation and reducing the impulsivity (or increasing the ability for self-control).

School Difficulties

In discussing the school difficulties that sometimes afflict HA children, it is important to emphasize that HA does *not* affect intelligence as ordinarily defined and measured by intelligence tests. The proportions of the bright, normal, and slow are the same among HA children as among children who are not HA.

Hyperactivity is not in any way related to mental retardation.

However, *some* HA children, not all, do have certain problems in intellectual development and in perception. Some may have an "unevenness" of intellectual development. Intelligence tests measure abilities and skills in a number of separate areas, such as vocabulary, arithmetic, understanding, memory, and certain forms of problem solving. Usually a child's performance is pretty much the same in each of these separate areas. If a child's vocabulary is normal for his age, his memory and problem solving are usually age-normal as well. HA children seem more likely to have uneven development. The child may be superior in vocabulary, average in memory, and somewhat slow in problem solving. His intelligence, which averages his ability in all these areas, may then be average but he may be advanced in some regards and behind in others. This may produce difficulties in school placement and adjustment. A hyperactive child in the third grade may be able to do fifth-grade mathematics, but only second-grade reading. If the school does not make allowances for these inconsistent abilities, the problems of such a child will be accentuated. He cannot be moved to a regular fifth or second grade, for he will be too slow for one and too fast for the other. Unless the school can arrange a program to take his abilities into account, he will not fit into *any* class.

Such children *sometimes* require special learning techniques and tutoring. In particular areas—for example, solving mathematical problems—they may have limitations that point to the advisability of diminished school demands. They may have difficulty learning the rules necessary to perform addition, subtraction, multiplication, and division. They may require many more repetitions than usual to learn the multiplication tables or the rules for long division. They may also tend to forget them rapidly. What the basic underlying problems are is unclear.

The area of perception, in which *some* HA children have problems, is a difficult area to define. It is more complex than simple seeing or hearing. It includes the abilities to distinguish between similar sights or sounds and the ability to put together sensations in a meaningful way.

For example, one perceptual task that sometimes gives a hyperactive child trouble is the problem of distinguishing between right and left. Young children have difficulty learning the difference between right and left and gradually learn to tell directions apart by the age of five or six. Young children confuse their right and left hands and feet and are apt to put their gloves on the wrong hands and their shoes on the wrong feet. Some HA children appear to be slow in learning the right-left concept (and a *very* few may also have problems in distinguishing between up and down). Problems in distinguishing between right and left seem associated with problems in reading.

Perceptual difficulties of this kind, and related difficulties, in children of normal intelligence, are called learning disabilities. Since they involve special educational problems of a substantial nature, we will describe them later in a special chapter.

We would like to repeat that many HA children have none of these perceptual problems. Even so, most HA children have considerable difficulty in learning at school. "Underachievement" is almost a hallmark of the HA child. Teachers and guidance counselors will, of course, recognize that the child has problems, and sometimes the school is the first place that the child's problems are clearly recognized. However, school personnel sometimes underestimate the problems related to hyperactivity and may attribute the child's difficulties to "emotional problems," "psychological maladjustment," or problems in the home.

If the HA child does *not* have specific perceptual problems, there are several possible explanations for his poor school performance. All his learning problems may stem from the attention difficulties and emotional overreactivity that have already been discussed. A hyperactive eight-year-old, despite normal intelligence, may be reacting to the school in the same fashion as a normal four- or five-year-old. Intelligence is not enough. A child must have the ability to concentrate for a reasonable period of time; he must hear at least *some* of what is said if he is to learn. He must have a reasonable amount of stick-to-itiveness and patience to tolerate difficult tasks; if he gives up immediately, learning will obviously be impaired. And, as has been mentioned several times, the HA child is both inattentive and readily frustrated. The learning problems are further complicated because they tend to move in vicious circles; they tend to snowball. His poor performance is apt to cause the teacher to say, either in so many words or indirectly: "Why can't you use your brains? . . . Why don't you finish your work? . . . Do your work. . . . You could if you wanted to." Thus poor performance leads to criticism, which in turn leads to the child's having a poor opinion of himself. Both are apt to decrease his motivation to do well. If he can't do well when he is trying to the best of his ability, he tends to give up. The result is a performance that grows steadily worse. If a child is a bit slow in the first few grades, he remains at a disadvantage even if most of the HA disappears and his learning ability catches up. Since he *is now* behind academically, school *is* harder and more frustrating.

Finally, much of any school experience is boring, tedious, repetitious. Many parents who visit an elementary school for the first time in ten or twenty years are impressed with its tedium and wonder how they were able to pay attention when they were children. This is not to say that making school into a consistently interesting experience would eliminate the HA child's difficulties. It very probably would not. We only mean to emphasize that the social structure in most schools makes the HA child's problems greater.

Difficulties in Coordination

Approximately half of HA children show various difficulties in coordination. Some HA children have limited "fine-motor control": they have trouble coloring, cutting with scissors, tying shoelaces, buttoning buttons, and writing. Others may have some mild difficulty with balance, for example, in learning to ride a bicycle. Still other HA children may have poor "hand-eye coordination": these children will be awkward in throwing and catching a ball or in playing baseball or tennis. Not all HA children have such problems. Many are well coordinated and some are excellent athletes. When coordination problems are present they usually cause more difficulties for boys than for girls because for boys athletic ability is an important source of acceptance by others. However, even the children with coordination handicaps may have no problems in activities requiring large muscle groups and may run or swim without difficulty.

Resistant and Domineering Social Behavior

Most hyperactive children manifest interpersonal behavior that has several distinctive characteristics: (1) a considerable resistance to social demands, a resistance to "dos" and "don'ts," to "shoulds" and shouldn'ts" (this is a frequent cause of difficulty with parents and teachers); (2) increased independence; (3) domineering behavior with other children.

Probably the single most disturbing feature of HA children's behavior, and the one most frequently responsible for their referral for treatment, is the difficulty many of these children have in complying with requests and prohibitions of parents and teachers. Some HA children may appear almost impossible to discipline. In some respects they seem to remain two years old. Parents describe them as "obstinate . . . stubborn . . . negativistic . . . bossy . . . disobedient . . . sassy . . . not caring." All the techniques of discipline seem unsuccessful: rewards, removal of privileges, physical punishment. "He wants his own way. . . . He never seems to hear. . . . He never learns by his own mistakes. . . . You can't reach him. . . . Punishment just rolls off his back. . . . He's almost immune to anything we do." HA children differ, however, in the ways that they manifest resistance. Some seem to forget what they are told, whereas others seem to oppose actively what is requested of them. We will discuss the meaning of this when we discuss the causes of the disorder.

With regard to independence, the HA child is often excessively independent but in a few instances he is excessively dependent. The independence may be noticed at an early age. The HA child is the sort of child who is apt to wander ten blocks away from home when he is two years old. When he is brought home to his terrified and angry parents, he is smiling and excited. He does not seem to get upset by the separation. He is *not* the sort of child who is likely to be upset the first few days of nursery school or kindergarten or when left with his grandparents. The few HA children at the other extreme, those who are excessively dependent, tend to be immature, babyish, and clinging. They are the children most apt to show the incessant attention-demanding behavior that has already been described.

The HA child's relationships with his brothers, sisters, and schoolmates are likely to follow a clearly recognizable pattern. When he is younger he is apt to be a tease. He becomes quite expert at getting others' goats, annoying, and bothering. As he grows older, he shows a very marked tendency to be bossy. Note how this contrasts with his refusal to be bossed by adults. When he plays with other children he strives to be the leader. He wants to decide what games are to be played. He wants to decide what the rules are, and if the game is not played the way he likes he may quit: he wants to play it his way or not at all. Needless to say, this does not win friends and influence people (at least favorably). Other children tend to avoid him, and after a while the HA child is likely to be without friends. This lack of friendship is much different from that which one sees in a shy, withdrawn child. The HA child is usually aggressive socially and *initiates* friendship successfully, but his style drives other children away. He will tell his parents that he is talked about, rejected, and perhaps even bullied. These reports are not excuses and they are not inaccurate. They are correct reports of what his own behavior compels other children to do. He "makes friends easily but can't keep them." As a result, the HA child often plays with younger children, and for the same reason the HA boy sometimes plays with girls. However, the HA child is not necessarily physically aggressive. He is not sadistic and he does not enjoy hurting others. He *does* tend to have more than his share of fights, but this is because of his impulsivity and because brothers and sisters and schoolmates are usually not enthusiastic about being pushed around and told what to do.

Emotional Difficulties

Most HA children show certain forms of emotional problems. The word *emotional* is one of those vague words used by everyone in a variety of different ways whose meaning is not clear. Let us emphasize first that calling these problems "emotional" does *not* imply that these problems are psychologically caused. Indeed, most of them are probably *not* psychologically caused.

HA children tend to have mood swings and cycles, so that their behavior tends to be unpredictable. Parents report: "He's happy one minute, impossible to get along with the next. . . . He has his good days and bad days, and it's hard to understand why." The last statement is worth emphasizing. All of us have our good and bad days, and often we can link our moods to our experiences. In the case of the HA child, it is usually more difficult to find out why he was bad yesterday and good today.

Many HA children are unusually underreactive and overreactive. They are sometimes insensitive to pain. They seem unaffected by and unreactive to the frequent bumps, falls, and scrapes that are the lot of younger children. (This is sometimes obscured by increased attention-seeking. When their parents are looking they may tend to squeeze out every last drop of sympathy obtainable.) They are often relatively fearless. A combination of this fearlessness, a craving for attention, impulsivity, and a tendency not to "plan ahead" is apt to land them in socially unapproved situations: when young, at the tops of trees; when older, impressing their adolescent peers with taboo behavior and inviting the interest of the local police. Fortunately, such fearlessness is *not* seen in all HA children.

The overreactivity of HA children sometimes manifests itself in excessive excitement during pleasant activities. Most young children will become excited at the circus, but HA children tend to become very overexcited in such circumstances. They even tend to lose control of themselves in less stimulating situations, for example, during a visit to a supermarket.

The overreactivity can also be seen in excessive irritability or anger during frustrating activities. Of course, most children, and adults, do not tolerate frustration or disappointment very well. But the HA child has a much lower tolerance for frustration and a more violent reaction to it. When things do not go his way he is subject to temper tantrums, angry outbursts, or sullen spells. Most young children become irritable and babyish when tired or hungry. An eight-year-old HA child may react to fatigue or hunger in the same way that a normal four-year-old does.

Although many parents describe their HA children as "angry," what they usually seem to be referring to is irritability rather than aggressiveness or hostility, that is, hyperreactivity to comparatively minor situations: "He's got a low boiling point . . . a short fuse. . . . When he is angry he loses control." Many HA children are described as being good-natured except during such outbursts.

One other characteristic that is seen in some HA children and is frequently disturbing to parents might be called "unsatisfiability." "He never gets a kick out of anything, at least not for long. . . . He can't be bothered to do much, nothing really seems to give him pleasure. . . . You can never satisfy him." This characteristic is sometimes produced by spoiling (in adults as well as children), but many HA children behave this way without ever having been spoiled. Their mothers may have noticed that they were not satisfiable from early infancy.

Finally, one "emotional" characteristic of most HA children is also seen in many children with other difficulties: low self-esteem. They have little self-confidence: "He doesn't think much of himself. . . . He thinks he's bad. . . . He thinks he's different." The cause and the treatment of this low self-esteem will be discussed later.

Immaturity

"Immaturity" is neither a very scientific nor a very specific word, but it often does accurately describe the behavior of HA children. Their lack of social, athletic, and academic skills, their inability to remember—and act on—"dos" and "don'ts," are certainly characteristic of younger children. The inability to tolerate frustration (resulting, often, in tantrums), the lack of stick-to-itiveness, are normal in younger children. Finally, *some* HA children have another trait associated with immaturity: rigidity, the inability to tolerate change (such children will be upset if their routine is changed, if the furniture in their room is rearranged, etc.). From a practical standpoint, it is often helpful for parents to remember that emotionally, *not* intellectually, their HA child may behave very much like a child four or five years younger than he is. Remembering this often makes it easier for parents to handle their child: many parents do not know how to act toward a nine-year-old with problems but do know how to deal with a normal four- or five-year-old. If the parents can remember that their HA nine-year-old is in *some* respects acting like a normal five-year-old, they may find it easier to understand and help him.

Changing Problems with Age

A salient aspect of the HA child's problems is that they tend to change as he grows older. The behavioral problems that are conspicuous in a toddler are very different from those that are conspicuous in an adolescent.

There are several reasons for this. First, there seem to be changes associated with maturation; for example, the hyperactivity itself tends to diminish with age (just as bed-wetting disappears with age). Second, there are changes that occur as a result of learning: the HA child is more hostile after his tenth year of rejection by schoolmates than he is after only one or two years of such treatment. Third, recognition of "problems" depends on one's understanding of the behavior considered normal for particular age groups: fidgety behavior is expected and tolerated in nursery school children but not in second graders; reading difficulty is expected in all first graders but is a problem in fourth grade.

What is the usual sequence of difficulties? In infancy the HA child's most conspicuous problems are in physiologic function: he is likely to be irritable, to have colic, and to have sleep disturbances. During the toddler stage his ability to do things increases immensely, and many of them are wrong things. The most disturbing traits are his continual getting into things and his inability to listen, that is, to respond to parental discipline.

As he reaches preschool age, his problems with attention and social adjustment achieve the limelight. His short attention span, low frustration tolerance, and temper tantrums make sustained play and nursery school participation difficult. Problems with his schoolmates soon appear: the teasing, domination, and other annoying behaviors. These qualities endear him neither to his teacher nor to his fellows, and in a few instances result in his beginning his academic career as a kindergarten dropout.

When he begins the first grade, his restlessness attracts attention: his teacher complains that he cannot sit still, that he gets up and walks around, whistles, and shuffles. Academic problems, though often present, tend to be ignored. First graders are not expected to read immediately. Bed-wetting may now appear. Although he may have always been a bed-wetter, bed-wetting is defined as a problem only when the child reaches an age when it is expected to disappear (usually about six), or when he stays overnight at camp or with friends. At about the third grade, when the child is nine or ten, academic and antisocial problems attract the most attention. Until that time slowness in school can be attributed to "immaturity" or academic unreadiness. But in the third grade the diagnosis is changed to "learning problem," or "learning disability." Reading difficulty causes the greatest concern, but the child may also have trouble with arithmetic and be criticized for messy writing. Outside of school, "antisocial behavior" is likely to be the cause of considerable concern. Both the duration and intensity of these problems are highly variable.

If the problems persist into early adolescence, the antisocial problems become the focus of attention. If academic problems persist, they may now be taken for granted. This is *not* to say that the *same* child who has a reading problem predictably develops social problems. Rather, if the child has both reading and social problems, the social problems are those that attract the greatest concern at this time.

We wish to emphasize very strongly that the age patterns that we have described do not apply to all HA children. Some children manifest difficulties in all developmental stages, some in only a few. At any one stage, the difficulties vary from child to child: some will have academic problems, some will have coordination problems, some will have learning problems, some will have social problems, some will have different combinations of these problems, and an unfortunate few will have all of them.

Finally, HA children tend to outgrow not only their hyperactivity but also many of the associated other difficulties. Any given HA child may follow the developmental sequence listed and then may no longer manifest HA characteristics at a later stage, say, as a preadolescent. In fact, it is not uncommon for the problems to diminish or become easily manageable at or around the time of puberty.

The combination of problems that are seen among HA children constitutes what is called a "syndrome" in medical terminology. A syndrome is a group of difficulties that *tend* to clump, cluster, or move together. It is characteristic of medical syndromes for a given individual *not* to have *all* the problems associated with the syndrome. It is also important to emphasize that the child who does not have some of the problems listed at any given stage in his development is very unlikely to develop them at a later stage. The child who does not have coordination problems when he is young will not get them when he is older. The child who does not have reading problems when he is seven or eight will not have them as a teen-ager. To the parents burdened with those difficulties that their HA child does have, this optimistic aspect of his development may be of some comfort. It is not to be minimized for it has been observed by physicians who have treated these children and worked with their families over periods of years.

3

The Causes of Hyperactivity

In virtually all instances hyperactivity is the result of an *inborn temperamental difference* in the child. How the child is treated and raised can affect the severity of his problem but it cannot cause the problem. Certain types of raising may make the problem worse, certain types of raising may make the problem better. *No* forms of raising can produce HA problems in a child who is not temperamentally predisposed to them.

Since child-rearing techniques can to some degree affect the seriousness of the HA child's problem, changes in these techniques are usually helpful. These will be discussed in the chapter on treatment. The fact that such psychological approaches can be helpful in the management of the HA child does not affect the explanation of the origin of the syndrome: the basic source of the difficulties seems to be inborn.

Causes of the Temperamental Problems

Knowledge about the causes of hyperactivity is very incomplete, but evidence from various scientific areas is beginning to fit together into a picture of an inborn constitutional deficiency. It is very important to emphasize first, as we mentioned earlier,

21

that *most HA children are not brain-damaged.* HA children are sometimes referred to as brain-damaged because HA was first described in children who had suffered injuries to the brain. The term *brain-damaged* not only is inaccurate but also is understandably upsetting to parents, who interpret it to mean that something is irreversibly the matter with the child's brain. We repeat, many brain-damaged children are not HA and most HA children are not brain-damaged. In the few instances in which brain damage *is* the cause, parents should be less pessimistic than they usually are. This will be discussed in the chapter on the development of the HA child.

If brain damage is not the cause, what is? There is recent scientific evidence supporting what everyone's grandmother knew: there are inborn temperamental differences among children. Studies of the growth of children from infancy to preadolescence reveal that children differ from their earliest days and that some of these differences tend to be associated with behavioral problems as the child grows up. For example, the difficulties that the HA child is likely to have in infancy (colic, feeding problems, sleeping problems) are probably the result of inborn temperamental differences. What causes these temperamental differences? Child psychiatrists are not certain. A very good possibility is that they are caused by chemical differences in the brain. The brain is an extraordinarily complex interconnection of nerve cells. It is in some ways analogous to a telephone network, but there is one major difference. In the telephone network the connections are *electrical:* electricity passes from one wire to another by physical contact. In the brain, however, the connections are *chemical.* One nerve cell releases a small amount of certain chemicals, which are picked up by a second cell, causing it to "fire." These chemicals are called "neurotransmitters." If there is too little of a particular neurotransmitter, the second cell will not fire because not enough of the neurotransmitter has been released by the first cell. Although the nerve cells themselves are intact, it is as if the connection were broken. There are different neurotransmitters in different portions of the brain. If the amount of one neurotransmitter is insufficient, the portion of the brain that it "operates" will not function correctly. HA children are probably deficient in some neurotransmitters. (In many HA children the quantity of these transmitters probably increases with age. This would seem to be the likely reason that the children improve as they grow older. This, too, will be discussed in the next chapter.)

The causes of these presumed chemical differences are, again, unknown but there are two general possibilities: (1) anomalies in the development of the baby *before* the time of birth; (2) genetic differences. Little is known about prenatal influences but there is some possibility that small birth size—and therefore prematurity—may sometimes lead to HA symptoms. Similarly, other variations in the mother's biological processes during pregnancy might result in fetal maldevelopment. With regard to genetic origins, it has long been observed that HA and reading problems sometimes run in families (and among the males usually, when they do). It has also been learned that such traits as hair color, eye color, certain forms of mental deficiency, etc., are related to the production of particular chemicals of the body, and that the amounts and types of these chemicals are determined by the genes—the transmitters of inherited characteristics. It may be that certain genes also control the amounts of neurotransmitters and that some genes result in too little production of the neurotransmitters. Neurochemists have some possible leads about which neurotransmitters may be insufficient in HA children. These chemicals are located in that portion of the brain that includes among its functions the regulation of attention. An *excess* of these neurotransmitters might produce an increased ability to focus attention and to inhibit behavior, to control oneself. A *deficiency* in these neurotransmitters—which is probably the condition present in HA children—would produce an underactivity of that portion of the brain, resulting in attention difficulties and some lack of self-control. This portion of the brain *probably* also acts to modulate the mood and to increase appropriate reactions to things going on outside the child. Therefore deficiency in neurotransmitters in this area would result in a decreased ability to focus attention; a decreased ability to check one's behavior—to apply brakes; a decreased sensitivity to others' reactions—to dos and don'ts, and approval or disapproval; and a decreased ability to modulate mood, that is, an increased tendency toward sudden and dramatic mood changes.

It is a common observation that particular kinds of temperament *tend* to run in families. In some families the children are high strung (like fox terriers or cocker spaniels), whereas in other families the children are more placid. Any temperamental characteristic is not an all-or-none trait. It is like height. There are all degrees of tallness, from the very short to the very tall. Most people who are very short or very tall do not suffer from a disease, although it may be very inconvenient to be 4'6" or 7'2". Similarly, most degrees of high-strungness do not cause problems unless they are excessive. All the traits of HA children that we have discussed occur in all children. At times, all children have short attention spans, are restless, are intolerant of not getting what they want. HA children have these characteristics to a marked degree. They are often, in a sense, extremes of the normal, as are very short or very tall people. Their characteristics are too much and too little of certain normal traits.

In families in which hyperactivity occurs on a temperamental basis, parents will frequently tell us that they had similar problems themselves when they were the age of their hyperactive son or daughter. Being aware that they had similar problems can be useful or harmful, depending on the circumstances. It can be an advantage when the parents remember the problems they faced and the techniques that were most helpful in dealing with them. This may provide useful insight for helping the child. The awareness can be harmful when the parents "play down" the difficulties hyperactivity may have caused them. If the parents are unwilling to acknowledge that hyperactivity caused them difficulty (or still does), they may minimize the problems it is causing the child. If this happens, the parents may neglect serious problems that require recognition if they are to be alleviated.

There are a number of other *possible* causes of hyperactivity of which physicians are only now becoming aware. The first is lead poisoning. It has been known for a long time that people who absorb too much lead develop both psychological and neurological (damage to nerves) problems. In fact, it was known thirty years ago that some children who ate lead (usually in the form of lead paint on walls, windowsills, or cribs) developed hyperactivity. What has recently been discovered is that lead poisoning may develop in children who have never consumed lead. Studies in big cities have suggested that some children who are diagnosed as hyperactive have mild, chronic lead poisoning. The reason for this is unknown. One very unpleasant possibility is that merely living in heavily trafficked areas and breathing air containing automobile fumes may be sufficient to develop lead poisoning. As everyone undoubtedly knows, a chemical compound containing lead has long been used in gasoline to improve the performance of cars. When the gasoline is burned, the lead becomes heated, becomes a gas, and passes into the air. In large cities, it may be sufficient merely to breathe the air to take in too much lead. Whether there is enough lead in the air in small- and medium-sized towns to allow for the same possibility is as yet unknown.

Another possible cause of hyperactivity has been proposed recently by a West Coast allergist (a physician specializing in the diagnosis and treatment of allergies, including such things as asthma, hay fever, and allergic reactions to foods), who has *claimed* that hyperactivity may be caused by the food children eat. Although these claims have received a great deal of publicity, they have been difficult to evaluate, in part because the claims themselves have changed. At first the doctor said that salicylates—chemicals related to aspirin that occur both in natural foods and in artificial colorings and flavorings—caused hyperactivity. Later, he claimed that salicylates were not important but that artificial food coloring—used in most processed foods—must be eliminated. It is important to realize that these claims have not been proven. A few preliminary experiments have been done and so far they have only indicated some areas that need further investigation. Some children apparently do improve when placed on a special diet, but the studies do not confirm that elimination of food colorings has anything to do with the improvement. Some children, for example, may benefit from the attention that comes from being placed on a special diet. It is hoped that additional studies, now being done, will clarify this issue in the future.

Another factor sometimes said to be a cause of HA is hypoglycemia, which means low blood sugar. To a physician, hypoglycemia is not present unless the blood sugar drops below a certain level, and if the blood sugar *is* below that level, it may indicate some underlying disease or disorder. Hypoglycemia defined in this way is a very uncommon condition. When the blood sugar does drop below a certain level, most people will have odd feelings, including light-headedness, a feeling of weakness, irritability, a cold sweat, and palpitations. They often feel anxious. Only the irritability reminds one of the symptoms of HA.

Despite the fact that hypoglycemia is uncommon, the diagnosis is frequently made. In many cases this is a mistaken diagnosis. The overdiagnosis of hypoglycemia may happen because some people experience mild changes, like those described above, when the blood sugar is low but still within the normal range. There is some evidence to suggest that experiencing these symptoms, even though the blood sugar is within normal range, occurs more frequently in people who are "nervous or high strung." Since HA children are frequently "nervous and tense," that may explain why many people think that HA children may have hypoglycemia. If a child experiences a worsening of behavior that seems to be related to what he eats, no harm will be done by altering the diet as long as one pays attention to basic nutrition. It would be wrong, however, to assume without further investigation that the child has the medical condition known as hypoglycemia.

Finally, some allergists have claimed that allergies to natural foods may cause HA. Children with definite food allergies sometimes develop what is known as the tension-fatigue syndrome. In this condition, the child develops symptoms of excess fatigue (which may be accompanied by an increase in motor activity and restlessness), increased irritability, and a resulting increase in "negative" behavior. When the food allergy is appropriately treated—and this means eliminating the offending food from the diet—the child's behavior also improves. However, the behavior typical of the tension-fatigue syndrome bears only a superficial resemblance to hyperactivity. Though the child may be more restless and irritable, he doesn't have the other symptoms that go along with HA. If the child already has HA *and* in addition develops a food allergy with accompanying behavioral changes, this can be expected to make his HA much worse. If the food allergy is treated, the HA child's behavior should also improve, but his HA problems will remain. Thus, although food allergy may worsen HA in some cases, there is no evidence to suggest that allergies cause HA.

Children with chronic hay fever also demonstrate behavioral changes when their hay fever is under poor control. They may become tired and irritable, with accompanying restlessness. Again, if the hay fever is successfully treated, their behavior often improves. Since hay fever is a common condition, many HA children can be expected to have this allergy in addition to their HA. If this is the case, treatment for the hay fever might be expected to help the child, but, again, it cannot be expected to eliminate completely his HA problems.

We have emphasized the importance of physiological contributions to hyperactivity for two reasons. First, many people are unaware of them. Second, they are the most common causes of the problem. In a *few* instances, they play a minor role. The size of the physiological contribution can vary. In some children they are very large, and no matter how the children are raised problems will appear. In other children there are only slight physiological contributions. With these children, problems will be minor unless there are substantial family problems. In these instances one usually finds that the child had done reasonably well until serious family problems arose. Sometimes one cannot be sure of the origin of the child's difficulties since serious family difficulties have been present at least since the time of the child's birth.

It is very important to note that no matter *how* the HA child's problems arise, they frequently lead to typical difficulties within the family. Some psychiatrists and psychologists see the family's stresses as being a *cause* of the HA child's problems. *Sometimes* they are. Very often they are not, but are, rather, understandable reactions to the burden of the child's unpredictable and difficult behavior.

Children, like adults, respond to distress in terms of their type of personality. HA children react by being moody, "naughty," restless. All families, of course, want to solve their internal problems; in families with HA children, some resolution of such conflicts becomes even more important.

Nature and Effects of the Temperamental Problems

In any given child it is impossible to say how much his personality and behavior are due to temperament ("nature") and how much are due to his life experience (to "nurture"). By the time he is six or seven his temperament has affected his behavior, which in turn has affected others around him, and their reactions in turn have affected him. For example, an aggressive child (not necessarily an HA child) will have bothered others, who in turn will have gotten angry, punished, and rejected him. The child feels rejected because he *has been rejected* (experience), but he has been rejected because he has been aggressive (temperament). Furthermore, a rejected child is more likely to feel frustrated and act aggressively. Temperament and experience snowball; they move in a vicious circle. The sorts of vicious circles that HA children get into will be discussed presently.

The central inborn temperamental differences of HA children include the following characteristic problems: (1) restlessness, (2) inattentiveness and distractibility, (3) demandingness, (4) impulsivity (the inability to inhibit oneself—to say "no" to oneself and follow through), (5) perceptual and learning difficulties, (6) social aggressiveness, and (7) hyperreactivity. These traits are *biologically caused*. They are *not* caused by the child's upbringing. However, these inborn traits affect experience and can also be affected by experience. The ways in which this can happen will be discussed below.

SCHOOL BEHAVIOR

Although school problems were discussed in the previous chapter, they are so common and so important that it may be useful to explain again how they arise. To repeat, distractibility, inattentiveness, lack of stick-to-itiveness, and special learning difficulties (when present) interfere with academic progress despite the presence of a normal I.Q. Even if the HA child does not have "special learning difficulties" or perceptual problems, he will have a harder time learning than his intellectual peers. To learn, a child must tolerate frustration. Some subjects are hard to understand and cannot be mastered without stick-to-itiveness. To learn, a child must pay attention. Intelligence is not enough. If the child cannot pay attention to what is being taught, he is, for all practical purposes, not there. To learn, a child must have patience. Elementary school requires a good deal of (boring) repetition, practice, and drill. A child who cannot force himself to complete tedious, disagreeable school tasks will have trouble in mastering reading, spelling, and arithmetic. The HA child is highly likely, therefore, to fall behind and become an under-achiever. As the child falls further behind, he will experience more frustration and criticism from teachers, parents, and fellow students. His parents will nag him for not doing his homework. He may be placed in a catch-up class or a "special learning disa-bility" class. He will regard himself as stupid and may be taunted as a "retard" by other children. Lack of success breeds low self-esteem and lack of enthusiasm. By the time he outgrows his distractibility and inattentiveness he may be so far behind and so soured on school that he only "wants out." Although he is now "normal" physiologically and the temperamental problems have diminished or disappeared, he is so scarred by school that he has acquired a marked distaste for it and may even drop out.

RELATIONSHIPS WITH OTHER CHILDREN

Because of his bossiness, his teasing, his "play it my way or not at all" attitude, the HA child is likely to be disliked by other children, and since he is not very sensitive to the feelings of others he may constantly do the "wrong" things. Even if he is not bossy, other problems associated with HA may interfere with his peer relations. If the child is a boy and has coordination prob-lems, the social problem will be worse. If he is chosen eighteenth when "choosing up" baseball teams, he will think little of him-self. If, in addition, he has a temper tantrum when he strikes out, his popularity will not go up. In order to be liked he may resort to a number of maneuvers that will get him into trouble with both children and adults. He may boast, brag, lie, clown, or show off. As he gets older, he may try to prove his worth by doing the most dangerous, and most self-destructive, things: stealing, climbing to the highest place, and so forth. Note how the temperamental characteristics (demandingness, hyperreactivity) lead to experience (rejection) that can lead to misguided attempts to improve relationships; the resultant social complications may reinforce the low self-esteem and make social interaction even more difficult.

In his relationships with his brothers and sisters, the same temperamental problems lead to other social difficulties. *All* brothers and sisters are jealous of one another from time to time. The HA child's behavior and the reactions that it produces in his parents predictably produce even more sibling envy and resentment than are common in any family. All the problems ordinarily associated with these sources of jealousies are aggravated and intensified. The HA child's brothers and sisters are probably favored because they are "good children" and he is "bad." They get more praise, he gets more blame, and he is jealous of them. On the other hand, he receives more attention than they—because he both demands it and requires it—and they may be jealous of him. Endless squabbling is often the result. Another, and unexpected, complication sometimes occurs if the HA child is treated and improves. The "good" children start showing "problems"! There are two explanations for this: first, they may previously have had problems but no one had noticed because the HA child's problems had been so much greater; second, the other children may have had no problems but have probably enjoyed their identification as the "good" children. When their HA brother or sister improves, they lose their enviable position and then manifest behavior that is very similar to the reactions of a child when a brother or sister is born. They may become jealous, act immaturely, and demand more attention. Fortunately this does not always happen. We mention it only because it is upsetting when it occurs unexpectedly and is less upsetting when one knows it *can* occur.

RELATIONSHIPS WITH PARENTS

The HA child's relationship with his parents is burdened by the difficulties encountered throughout his development. It will be recalled that because of his *temperamental* problems, the HA child tends to be unsatisfiable from infancy. The mother cannot stop his colic, cannot handle his sleep disturbances, cannot satisfy him or make him happy. As he grows older, his hyperreactivity, his impulsivity, and the other behavior problems we have discussed add tensions to family life. Nothing the parents seem to do helps very much or for very long. As already mentioned, probably the most common parental complaint is the difficulty in disciplining the HA child. The child is inattentive and rapidly forgets. When told to eat with his fork, he complies, but his mind soon wanders off and he is again eating with his hands. He is told to clean his room, but when he is half finished (or one-tenth finished), he starts doing something else. He is told *not* to jump down the stairs, stops for a while, and impulsively does it again. He is *not totally* unresponsive to discipline. But he is *much less* responsive than non-HA children. If parents are *very firm* and *very consistent* they will find the HA child can be disciplined—at least to some extent. *If* they are *not* firm and *not* consistent, they may find that he is almost totally out of control. How he is handled will *often* (not always) make a large difference. This is obviously of great importance in management and will be discussed in the pertinent chapter.

The difficulty in controlling the HA child's impulsivity has several disturbing effects. First, the child is a disappointment. Second, the child's chronic misbehavior is likely to make the parents angry. Third, the parents may see themselves as inept and inadequate. These feelings bring further emotional complications because the parents believe that they are not "supposed" to feel chronically angry toward their children. There are many emotions that people are not supposed to feel. One should not hate one's parents or one's child, or envy one's sister. But such feelings do arise, and when they do, people tend to suppress them. They pretend they are not there, they ignore them, they refuse to acknowledge them. Usually people are successful in these attempts and *most* of the time they are unaware that these feelings exist. Every now and then, however, in everyone, such feelings break through. When they do, one is apt to feel bad and guilty. When the parents of the HA child become aware of their angry feelings, they feel even more inadequate, and guilty and depressed as well. These feelings not only are highly distressing, but also are likely to lead to techniques of child rearing that will aggravate the HA child's problems. Since reward and punishment seem ineffective in discipline, the parents are already confused, frustrated, and baffled. The anger the child engenders may make the parents act with excessive harshness. They may remove bicycle or TV privileges for a week. They may spank the child a little too hard. The parents' awareness of their severity (to a small child!) tends to produce further guilt, which leads them to try to atone by being more lenient. Frequently this leads to a pattern of alternating excessive discipline and excessive permissiveness, a pattern that is the opposite of the *consistent* atmosphere in which the child functions best. The "catch" is that it is the child's behavior that is likely to make his parents behave *inconsistently*.

As a further complication, severe and harsh discipline (which is very different from *firm* discipline) can produce certain kinds of "problems," or maladjusted behavior, in *any* child, and these responses sometimes appear in the HA child. Someone weak who feels he is being treated too harshly will feel resentful. But he has only limited ways of fighting back. He may comply resentfully, doing the job to the letter but not in the spirit of the law. He may merely pretend to comply. He may, at the risk of further punishment, dig in his heels and be negative, ornery, or stubborn. He may attempt to strike back by doing annoying, naughty, or hurtful things in another area. Nobody likes always being told what to do and what not to do. Even if the parent is a saint, the HA child (who finds it difficult to inhibit himself) will feel as if he is receiving more than his share of dos and don'ts and will be more inclined to stiffen his back in protest.

This friction leads to problems in other areas. As the parent-child problems multiply, the HA child will feel angry at his parents, but if one expresses anger at a loved one, one runs the risk of driving the loved one away. So in some cases the anger may not be expressed very directly. It can spill over and get taken out on a relatively innocent bystander, such as a playmate or teacher. The anger can also be completely bottled up. In adults this may be associated with psychosomatic disorders. For example, a person may keep his feelings inside himself but grow tense; in some instances he may actually get spasms and pains in his muscles (as expressed in the phrase "you give me a pain in the neck"). Lastly, the anger may be taken out on the child himself. This phenomenon is most surprising from the common-sense point of view but is frequently seen in very angry and inhibited adults. They will have accidents and hurt themselves; they will engage in behavior that results in humiliation or punishment. The same kind of behavior can sometimes be seen in the HA child.

To further compound and complicate the difficulties, the child's behavior often causes disagreement and dispute between the parents. Both parents perceive the child as behaving poorly, and each tends to blame the other for disciplining or treating the child inadequately. In particular, the father is apt to notice that he is more effective in controlling the child. He is, of course, less frequently around the home, and when he appears he is likely to lower the boom, with the result that the child heaves to, at least briefly. The father's natural remark to his wife is: "I can control him—why can't you?" His wife, who spends much more time with the child, replies: "You can't treat him like that all day long," and the fight is on. Many parents have different views on how much strictness and severity are necessary in discipline. A parent whose own experience as a child has been with harsh discipline tends to favor this approach, and one whose experience has been gentler is likely to oppose it. Consequently, one sometimes sees the formation of family "triangles." One parent will be cast in the role of the child's defender while the other becomes the prosecutor. The prosecutor parent, who is the "odd man out," then has an additional problem. Not only does he (or she) have a difficult child, but also his (or her) spouse is siding with the child against him. The parent who has been "pushed out" then feels jealous of his own child. Again, jealousy is one of those feelings that parents are not "supposed" to have, but do. Brief reflection about one's own family or the families of friends should quickly bring to mind numerous illustrations of the complications, animosities, and guilt that can ensue.

There is another and almost universal familial complication. In the recent past almost all child psychiatrists and psychologists have maintained that most of the behavioral problems seen in children were the results of the manner in which they were raised by their parents. Most parents who have done any reading on child rearing are aware of these notions, but are not aware that they are becoming very much out of date. Such parents reach what they think is an obvious conclusion. They have a child with behavior difficulties. Children's behavior difficulties are the results of their parents' difficulties. Therefore, the parents—they themselves—must be either stupid or evil. Their child's difficulties are not only a serious problem in themselves, but are also a reflection of the parents' failure as parents. Unfortunately, many mental health workers may reinforce the parents in this view of themselves. A substantial number of psychiatrists, psychologists, social workers, teachers, and school guidance counselors are unaware of the evidence for the physical basis of the problem of hyperactivity. They, too, believe that the child's problems are a reflection of his parents' problems. They will inform the parents, subtly or otherwise, that they are responsible for the child's difficulties. This will either intensify the parents' sense of guilt, anxiety, and depression, or lead them to deny that there is anything wrong with the child. The latter course would be difficult to follow, but rather than be labeled as bad parents of a bad child, some people will deny the evidence of their senses and proclaim that their child is perfectly normal but misunderstood by others. This is an understandable, common, and unfortunate technique that delays or prevents the problem from being solved. Many parents of HA children have accused themselves for many years, and a final prosecution by experts may lead them to defend themselves by denying the existence of problems in the child, which in turn leads to the child's not receiving treatment. The important point we wish the reader to take away is that, contrary to usual belief, family disturbances are often the result and not the cause of a child's problems.

Certainly these parent-child sequences are not seen in all families with HA children and not even in most of them. They have been presented to illustrate how temperament in the child can produce changes in those around him, which in turn will produce psychological changes in the child. Notice that the temperament of the parent is very important in this equation. If the parent is hot-tempered or impulsive, because of either temperament or experience, he or she is more apt to become involved with and intensify the child's problems.

THE CHILD'S FEELINGS ABOUT HIMSELF

Although the HA child sometimes feels anger in response to his parents' reactions to his behavior, he more often has other reactive feelings that are more self-destructive. Because the child is rejected, is criticized, is told he is exasperating, he will feel unlovable and unworthy, and think little of himself. Parental self-control can diminish these feelings but it cannot prevent them. Even though he is somewhat thick-skinned and even though people may say nothing, the child cannot help noticing how they react to him.

Obviously, anything that can help the child change his behavior will prevent him from suffering the consequences of his behavior. The consequences of his temperamentally determined behavior are of the utmost importance for the child's psychological development. Although a child may eventually outgrow the physiological and the temperamental problems, the psychological difficulties he has had because of the temperamental problems may persist. He will have learned—and not forgotten—patterns of psychological maladjustment. On the other hand, if the physiological problems and symptoms can be kept in check until he outgrows them, he will avoid many bad experiences and grow up more easily. He will be better in school and have better relationships with his family and friends. He will not suffer severe consequences from his hyperactivity. Many HA children can now be helped to achieve this major goal, as will be discussed in the chapter on treatment.

4

The Development of the Hyperactive Child: The Outcome of Hyperactivity

In the chapter on the characteristics of the HA child, we discussed the changes in his problems as he grows. We also mentioned that the sequence of problems is not inevitable, and many HA children grow out of their problems as they become older. An obvious and reasonable question that the parents might ask is what the fate of their HA child will be. This question is not easy to answer. The usual scientific way of answering such a question is to look through case records of people diagnosed as having the ailment several years ago, and then to evaluate the same patients at the present time. This procedure is difficult to follow with hyperactivity since the syndrome has only recently begun to be widely recognized. If one does look through old records, one will not find children who have been diagnosed as HA. One will find children who one suspects would have been diagnosed as HA if hyperactivity had been well known several years ago. Since adequate old case records are not available, we will have to wait several years to see the developmental course of children who have currently been diagnosed as hyperactive.

Nevertheless, we are not totally in the dark. We do have information from two sources. The first source consists of psychiatrists who have been treating HA children for many years. The second consists of studies of severely disturbed HA children who were identified and labeled many years ago. The second source of information is likely to be misleading since it refers to a very small segment of HA children, those rare HA children whose problems were unusually severe.

Physicians who have treated HA children over a period of years have repeatedly noted that the problems tend to change, to become less severe, and to disappear with age. It is this sort of progress that has caused come physicians to label the problem a "developmental lag." (The implication is that the HA child, who is immature, is like a child who is unusually short for his age. Both are likely to catch up, to become mature or taller, but later than most children.) In many HA children some of the more troublesome symptoms gradually diminish and finally disappear around the time of puberty; in some children such improvements may occur earlier and in some later. In all HA children some symptoms change and disappear. The HA child may wet his bed longer than the nonhyperactive child, but he does not wet his bed forever. Similarly, restlessness and fidgetiness diminish with age. However, and this is extremely important, even though these symptoms may vanish, other HA symptoms may persist. Difficulty in concentrating, lack of stick-to-itiveness, and impulsivity may remain. In talking to adults who had HA problems in their youth one frequently hears that it was not until late adolescence or early adulthood that they finally settled down. Obvious hyperactivity disappeared whereas many of the other problems lingered for several years. The practical consequence is that treatment, when effective, may need to be continued for several years after the most obvious and distressing symptoms have vanished.

In considering the practical implications of the development of the HA child, one must ask this question: "Is the persistence of symptoms due to the persistence of the temperamental (biochemical) problem, or is the persistence due to maladjusted patterns of behavior that were learned because of the (no longer existing) temperamental problem?" The question cannot be answered in a general way, but a sensitive clinician can often give an approximate answer for an individual child. In some children, the problems do seem to persist because of the persisting temperamental difficulty. In other children the persistence of symptoms seems to be the result of behavior that was learned and now remains, so to speak, as a habit. (Similarly, a child who had broken his right arm and learned to write with his left hand might well retain indefinitely the ability to write with his left hand even after the fracture healed.)

The temperamental difficulty often responds well to medical treatment. This will be discussed in the next chapter. Learned behavior is not so easy to change, particularly if it is learned in early life. For example, children exposed to a foreign language before they are five or six learn it more easily and remember more of it than does an intelligent adult. Habits and attitudes, like skills, are learned more quickly and better when young, and habits learned when young are harder to unlearn. Further, some personality traits and attitudes developed in adolescence can be very durable, so it is desirable that the child have every possible physical and psychological advantage as he approaches that period. For example, in one study thin women who had been fat in childhood or in adolescence were asked how they regarded themselves. Interestingly, only those women who had been fat in adolescence had suffered psychological effects and continued to regard themselves as unattractive despite the fact that they were thin. Attitudes learned during the teen-age years had stuck with them. The relevance for HA children is, we hope, obvious. The sooner that maladaptive learning can be prevented, the better, for the child will have less difficulty in adolescence and later life than he would have otherwise. If such habits or attitudes are learned, the outlook is not grim. Learned habits can be unlearned, skills can be acquired, new experiences can change personality throughout one's life—and the chapter on treatment will consider some psychological approaches that are pertinent here. But from what we know about children's growth and development, *early prevention would seem to be more effective than later treatment.*

Recently, a number of researchers (including PHW) have discovered that in some unfortunate persons many hyperactive problems persist until the thirties or forties. We first became aware of this by talking to the parents of many HA children. Frequently the parents mentioned that they had been hyperactive in childhood and that the problems had become less severe with age but still bothered them to an annoying degree. These adults differed from HA children not only in that many of the problems were less severe than they had been, but also in that the parents had developed adult ways of coping with their problems. Of particular interest—and of practical importance—was our discovery that many of the adults who continued to suffer from HA problems continued to benefit from treatment with medications as much as did HA children. These findings are very new and must be confirmed by other scientists. If these findings are verified, they mean that we should look for persistent HA in some adults and that we may be able to treat it with the same techniques that are beneficial to HA children.

Similarly, learning disabilities may persist well into the thirties and forties. Although *apparently* (there is no really substantial information) "spurts" naturally occur at around age eight and in the early teens, during which learning disabilities improve, there is an overall tendency for learning disabled children to fall further and further behind with age. We *believe* that perhaps one-third of learning disabled children continue to have serious problems well into adult life. In the other two-thirds some improvement occurs, but learning disabled children often continue to be slow readers and poor spellers, and if they have had difficulty with arithmetic, they continue to have problems in performing arithmetical calculations.

The above statements may be disheartening. Physicians are somewhat less optimistic about HA and learning disabilities than they need to be. We know that *without* treatment the number of children who continue to have problems is larger than was previously believed. It is our *hope* that early and well-administered psychological treatment, in combination with appropriate medication if indicated, may prevent—or greatly reduce—the psychological symptoms that develop on the basis of the physiological abnormalities. Such treatment, of course, does not cure the underlying physiological abnormalities, and perhaps the reason that some treatment programs in the past proved ineffective may simply be that they did not administer medication long enough. Since we now have evidence that some HA children continue to have the same "physiological" difficulties in adult life (inattentiveness, hot temper, not being able to complete tasks, and so on) and continue to respond to medication, it seems obvious that some HA children may benefit from—and may need to take—medicine for many years after childhood. How many HA children fall into this category we do not know, but, again, it is many more than was previously believed.

The developmental picture that we have been discussing has emerged largely from reports by physicians with extensive clinical experience with a great range of HA children. The other major source of information—old studies of severely disturbed HA children—is not very illuminating with regard to most HA children since it largely deals with those few whose difficulties are profound. These studies have shown that profoundly disturbed HA children are more likely to have serious psychiatric disorders in later life. It is obvious that this small group of children should receive continuing treatment from an early age.

At this point, and almost as an aside, something should be said about brain damage and hyperactivity. As was emphasized, documented brain damage is not the cause of most cases of HA. When brain damage is related to HA, it generally appears to be damage sustained around the time of birth or during pregnancy. At present we do not know if the subgroup of HA children who do have such damage are subject to a developmental course that is different from that experienced by other HA children. Most people regard brain injury as permanent and irreversible, but this is because our usual experience is with brain injury in adults. There are differences in the effects of such injury at different periods of life, however. It might be reassuring to mention some of the things that are known about the effects of brain injury in very early life. The most important fact is that very early injury can often be compensated for. Although the young, like the old, cannot grow new brain cells, they sometimes can adjust to brain injury quite well, apparently because the functions of the damaged areas are taken over by other portions of the brain. This can be illustrated by some experiments on monkeys. If a certain part of the brain of an *adult* monkey is removed he will behave as if he had a stroke: one side of his body will be paralyzed (or weak) and uncoordinated. If the same portion of the brain of an *infant* monkey is removed he will have difficulties at first but *over time* he will recover complete function: he will not be weak or uncoordinated on one side of his body. Obviously there are no similar experiments on children but the implication is clear. One can hope for more recovery from an injury in the young than from the same injury in the old.

To summarize, first, *many* HA children, particularly those whose symptoms are not severe, outgrow their symptoms at or around the time of puberty. Second, *some* HA children lose some of their symptoms at puberty (for example, restlessness) but may continue to have other symptoms (for example, impulsivity and poor concentration) for several years thereafter. All these children *may* suffer some psychological effects from their temperamental problems, and treatment should be considered for them at least until they outgrow the temperamental symptoms. For children in whom some temperamental problems linger, it may be helpful to continue treatment for several more years.

5

Treatment of the Hyperactive Child

The treatment of the HA child is often relatively simple. It almost always requires the services of a physician. Since, as will be discussed below, medication is of the greatest importance in most instances, nonmedical specialists, such as psychologists, educators, and social workers, cannot assume primary responsibility for treatment. They may provide useful and sometimes absolutely necessary assistance, but since they are not trained to use and cannot prescribe medications, they are unable to supply the treatment that is both the best and *sometimes* the *only* treatment required. This must be emphasized because too often the HA child or his family is referred to a psychologist, social worker, or school guidance counselor. Such referrals are made because of psychological maladjustment in the child, problems in the family, or failure in school. These problems, as we have said, may be a *result* of hyperactivity in the child, and they may also worsen hyperactivity in the child. Some, particularly family problems, may be largely irrelevant.

What frequently happens is that the HA child is misdiagnosed and referred for help, and it is then noticed that his parents have marital problems. Someone then assumes that the child's problems are the result of family problems, and the parents receive treatment. This happens frequently because the traditional view in child psychiatry has been that most children's problems are the product of their parents' or their families' problems. The difficulty is that a large number of married couples have serious problems. An increasingly large proportion of all marriages end in divorce. Of those that do not, perhaps half have serious difficulties. Thus, the chances are great that the parents of any child are having difficulties. If one looked at the parents of children with rheumatic fever, epilepsy, or mental retardation, one would find that the majority of them had marital problems. (And, in fact, some of these problems might be caused by the child's illness.) No one would expect that helping the parents would cure a child's rheumatic fever, epilepsy, or mental retardation. Helping the parents might, and probably would, make the child happier. Similarly, it is quite possible that the parents of an HA child are having marital difficulties; if one helps only the parents, the child will probably be more comfortable in some ways, but his basic problems will remain untouched and unchanged. A major difficulty for the HA child is that his problems are often not recognized as medical. His medical problems manifest themselves in his behavior, and until recently all such problems were thought to be psychologically caused. The reasoning has been that if he has "psychological" problems, his parents, and perhaps he himself, require only psychological treatment. Simple—and very incorrect. Normal children may have disturbed parents. Disturbed children may have normal parents. Disturbed children may have disturbed parents and the two sets of disturbances may be largely separate.

The same observations that apply to psychological help for family problems apply in part to the individual psychological treatment of the HA child, or child psychotherapy. Almost all HA children have psychological problems. *Sometimes* these can be helped by psychotherapy. But as long as the temperamental problems remain, the psychological problems will continue to spring up. In other words, the young HA child—and the adolescent child in whom temperamental problems remain—will require treatment for those temperamental problems. Psychotherapy may benefit the child—and later we will discuss how—but unless he is medically treated it is very likely that he will develop new problems.

Finally, the same principles hold for educational treatment. The school counselor will see the child with educational problems or behavioral problems or both. He may assume that the behavioral problems are causing the academic ones, or that the academic problems are causing the behavioral problems. He is probably *partly* right in either case. The catch is that both kinds of problems can be separately caused by hyperactivity. Dealing with either without treating the underlying hyperactivity may be helpful but it is not the best treatment.

To repeat, the help provided by trained professionals other than physicians can be important and sometimes necessary to the HA child and his family, but most HA children *require* medical treatment; at present only physicians are in a position to provide such treatment. Once the child has embarked on the basic course of medical treatment, it will be easier to decide whether the parents should also seek help for him from a psychologist, social worker, or teacher.

All three major forms of treatment will be discussed in this chapter: the medical, psychological, and educational. We will also add a few words about help for the youngster whose hyperactivity is discovered in adolescence.

Medical Treatment

A very large fraction of HA children can be helped, often to a marked degree, by treatment with medication. In some children this may be the *only* treatment that is required. In others psychological and educational treatment may also be necessary. As mentioned, it is often difficult beforehand to determine how much of a child's trouble is caused by family difficulties, and how much by his own temperament. Often, after a child has been treated with medications some of the problems may disappear while others will remain. At times like this the physician may suggest psychological treatment for the family and/or the child and/or educational treatment for the child.

The use of medication to treat children is sometimes upsetting to parents. Parents are upset for various reasons and it may be useful to discuss them.

First, many parents have difficulty coming to terms with the fact that their child's behavior problems have a "physical" rather than a "psychological" basis; often this is because they find physical problems frightening. They feel that in the area of behavior what is psychological can easily be remedied whereas what is physical cannot. They feel that a temper tantrum is soon over, but the damaged brain may never recover. For this reason they would rather believe that the problem is psychological. If the child's misbehavior is psychological, surely the powerful psychiatrists can change it, but how can his brain be "cured"? On both counts the parents' information is incomplete. Fortunately, just as with many other serious physical problems, behavior malfunctions with physical origins can sometimes be easily remedied. On the other hand, psychological treatment is by no means as effective as it is sometimes believed to be. Certain common forms of brain tumor that cause profound psychological disturbances can be easily removed, whereas, in contrast, certain forms of neurosis of psychological origin cannot be cured despite years of expensive and time-consuming psychological treatment. Pneumonia can often be cured with a single shot of penicillin. Pernicious anemia, formerly a fatal disease, can be completely cured by vitamin administration. But a child who has been neglected and psychologically abused during early childhood may never function normally even if he later receives warm, considerate parental care and psychotherapy.

A second reason parents sometimes object to treatment with medication is that treatment with medication seems "artificial." To many parents it does not seem to be a good way to get to the root of the problem. That may be so if the root of the problem is psychological, but in this case the root of the problem is generally physical. Because certain portions of the brain are not functioning adequately their function must be restored through chemical means. Medication can be looked on as a form of replacement therapy; that is, it apparently supplies chemicals that are lacking or causes the body to create more of the chemicals that are lacking. At present, we can give no chemical that will permanently cure the deficiency. Unlike pneumonia, hyperactivity has no one-shot cure. Medication is necessary until the brain, through its own growth and development, begins producing adequate amounts of the required chemicals. This is very similar to the treatment required for pernicious anemia, except that the pernicious anemia requires administration of vitamin B_{12} throughout the patient's life; unlike the hyperactive child, the patient with pernicious anemia never outgrows his difficulties.

A third reason parents sometimes object to medication is that they fear that the child will become dependent on it. By dependency, parents generally mean two things. First, the parents fear that the medication is related to the substances currently feared as "drugs." They sometimes fear that, like the drug addict, the child will feel so good after taking the medication that he will become addicted to it. This is never true of the medications employed by physicians in the treatment of hyperactivity. Children may be happy about the improvement in their lives that medicine helps to produce but they never like the medicine. They do not get "high" from it. They do not get "kicks" from it. Medically, any non-naturally occurring substance that is administered to a person with the hope of therapeutic results is a drug. Aspirin is a drug. Penicillin is a drug. Certain forms of hormones are drugs. The problem is not whether a substance is a medication or a drug, but whether it is beneficial or harmful. As will be seen, most of the medications used in the treatment of hyperactivity are beneficial and carry very little risk.

A second form of dependency that parents sometimes fear is the need for constant medication to handle problems. In this respect the parents are correct, but the dependency is preferable to the ailment. Many hyperactive children *do* need medicine to control their problems. The hyperactive child is in a position similar to that of the child with diabetes, epilepsy, or rheumatic fever. Children with those disorders must take insulin, anti-epileptic drugs, or penicillin for the rest of their lives. The hyperactive child is luckier. He will have to take medication for only a part of his life.

In discussing the major medications employed by most physicians in the treatment of HA children, their effects, and their administration, our aim will be to help the parent understand the physician's treatment goals. We will not be presenting an exhaustive list of medications, and of course the discussion is not intended to enable parents to treat their child by themselves. Parents who are aware of how a drug should act, what side effects it can produce, and what (if any) possible hazards accompany its use, are in a much better position to assist their physician in the treatment of their child. With this in mind, let us now turn to some general aspects of the administration of medication to HA children.

The first very important point to be made is that several medications are potentially helpful for children with HA. It is impossible to predict how a child will respond to a particular medication. Some children respond very well to one medication and not to another. It may be necessary to try several before the best one is found.

A second important point is that sometimes the medication does not take effect immediately but seems to require a cumulative buildup in the body, so that it is necessary for a child to be on the medicine for some time before one can decide how effective it can be. Sometimes this period may be as long as several weeks. In a few instances the medicine will at first seem to make the child's symptoms worse; parents should be aware of this so that they will not stop the medication immediately. In these few instances, after a week or two of deterioration, a child's symptoms and problems *may* then begin to get better.

Another important principle is that in beginning any course of medication the physician will start at the smallest dose that is *ever* effective, since he does not wish to give more medication than is necessary. Because he starts with a small dose it is often necessary to increase the amount of medicine considerably. This should be no cause for alarm. Children differ greatly, and some children need much larger amounts of medication than do other children. The amount of medication they need is not necessarily related to the seriousness of the problem. Some extremely hyperactive children need only very small amounts of medicine whereas some children who are much less hyperactive require larger amounts.

Another point to bear in mind is that many medications produce side effects. A side effect is an undesired by-product of the administration of medicine. For example, aspirin sometimes produces irritation of the lining of the stomach and mild abdominal pain. Antihistamines, given for hay fever, sometimes produce sleepiness. The medications used in treating HA children will *sometimes* produce in some children a number of side effects. When we discuss the individual medications, we shall mention these side effects.

Lastly, all medicines may produce allergic reactions. An allergic reaction occurs only in some people who receive medication. Some medications are much more likely to produce allergies than others. The drugs most commonly used in treating HA children, the stimulant drugs, very rarely produce allergies. Some medications that are used when the stimulant drugs do not seem to be the best treatment for an individual child are somewhat more likely to produce allergies. (It should be remembered that all medicines, and this includes aspirin and penicillin, can produce allergies.) The parents should know the symptoms of allergies and should contact the doctor if they do occur. They are rare, but if allergies are allowed to go on, they sometimes become worse. Some of the major symptoms are quite obvious: skin rash, hives, etc. One other major symptom of allergy, of which many people are not aware, is a decrease in white blood cell count, which results in an increased susceptibility to infections. When such an allergy occurs it is most common for a person to develop a sore throat and a high fever. Of course, most children who are not receiving medications of any sort occasionally get sore throats and high fevers, but a child who is receiving medication and develops such symptoms should immediately be seen by a physician.

STIMULANT DRUGS

The drugs most frequently used in the treatment of HA children are the stimulant drugs. The most common of these are d-amphetamine (several trade names, of which perhaps the most common is Dexedrine) and methylphenidate (trade name: Ritalin).

Amphetamine was first used for the treatment of HA children in 1937. Methylphenidate has been used since the early 1960s. A less common drug, pemoline (trade name: Cylert), has been available in Europe for a number of years but has only recently been introduced into the United States. These are generally the most effective and safest medicines available in the treatment of HA children. Approximately two-thirds of HA children respond well to one of these drugs. Although the drugs are approximately equal in effectiveness, a particular child may respond better to one than to another. If one drug provides only moderate improvement or produces annoying side effects, a physician may then try another.

Despite their effectiveness and safety, amphetamines and methylphenidate have recently acquired a bad reputation because they may cause *adults* to become "high" and psychologically dependent upon them. (Amphetamine is well known as "speed.") Pemoline does not appear to have this property, and although it has been available in Europe for some time, little or no abuse has occurred. However, like the amphetamines and methylphenidate, it is stimulating to normal adults. Stimulant drugs have a much different effect in HA children then they do in normal adults. Rather than becoming high or excited, HA children are in general calmed down by these drugs and sometimes (rarely) they may even become somewhat sad. Children do not become addicted to these medications; there is absolutely no danger that this will occur. If the HA child's problems persist into adolescence, many physicians will discontinue the use of the stimulant drugs and substitute medications that are not habit-forming in adults. However, many physicians who have treated numerous HA children may continue to use the stimulant drugs well into adolescence—with caution—because of their medical impression that these children do not begin to respond to the drugs as do normal adults until they have outgrown their HA problems.

The HA adults we have treated so far—and their number is still small—have generally shown the same response to medication that HA children do. They become, as we shall discuss further below, calm rather than excited, and they do not become "high." Furthermore, the HA adults we have treated continue to benefit from the same relatively small doses. This contrasts with adults who abuse stimulant drugs for their pleasant effects, who must escalate the dosage, sometimes to a hundred times as much, to continue to receive the drug effect.

1. Effects

When the stimulant drugs are effective, HA children generally become calmer and less active, develop a longer span of attention, become less stubborn, and are easier to manage. In addition, they frequently become more sensitive to the needs of others and much more responsive to discipline. It should be emphasized that these effects are very different from those of the so-called "tranquilizing" drugs. Tranquilizing drugs may slow a child down but they do not increase his attention span, personal sensitivity, or reasonableness.

When the stimulant drugs are effective, they produce unusually dramatic results. For the duration of their action they appear to make the child more psychologically mature in a variety of areas. When they do work they produce one of the most dramatically effective responses that can be seen in psychiatry. When the amphetamines and methylphenidate are effective, they usually are effective immediately. In a few instances, the effects described may take as long as a week or two to appear. The effects of pemoline are seen much more slowly: it may take two or three weeks for pemoline's full benefit to be realized. As mentioned, occasionally a child taking stimulant drugs will appear to be worse at first—he may become more irritable and more active. In quite a few (not all) of these cases, if he continues to receive medication, this effect goes away and he becomes calmer.

2. Dosage

Parents' evaluation of their child's adjustment will play an important role in the doctor's decision to increase or decrease the dose of the medication. The parents should know something about the dosages ordinarily employed. Medications are usually measured in milligrams. A milligram (one-thousandth of a gram) is a unit of weight, about 1/30,000th of an ounce. The amount of dextroamphetamine (*d*-amphetamine) an HA child may require usually ranges from about 5 to 60 milligrams a day. The amount of methylphenidate an HA child may require may range from 10 to 120 milligrams a day. Pemoline, which comes in odd dosages, is usually prescribed in amounts between 18.75 and 112.5 milligrams per day. There are occasional exceptions, in either direction: a very few children will require less than these dosages, and a few will require more.

Dextroamphetamine is available in two forms: tablets and long-acting capsules. The tablets generally last from 3 to 6 hours, whereas the long-acting form of the medicine lasts anywhere from 8 to 16 hours. The advantage of the long-acting form is that the child need only receive medicine once a day, in the morning; in contrast, the tablets usually have to be given two or three times a day. For reasons mentioned below, however, the use of the long-acting form of medication is not always possible. Methylphenidate is available only as tablets.Its effects are somewhat shorter, perhaps lasting 3 or 4 hours. For this reason it is often given two or three times a day (morning, noon, and, perhaps, early afternoon). The effects of pemoline vary. In some children it seems to last approximately 12 to 18 hours, while in others its effect may carry over through the next day and perhaps even longer.

If the child is taking a medication whose effects last only 3 or 4 hours, and does not come home from school for lunch, the medication must be administered around noon at school. In some schools the nurse can do this, although many children do not want to visit the nurse because they are afraid the other children will identify them as being different. Many children assume responsibility themselves for taking their medicine at school. The task is easiest if the child brings his lunch to school rather than buying it in the cafeteria. The medication can be wrapped separately—for example, in a small piece of aluminum foil—and packed with the sandwich. The drug can also be carried in a pocket, but if the child is a chronic forgetter, it may be impossible to use short-acting drugs such as methylphenidate. In such instances, one may have to switch to long-acting drugs such as dextroamphetamine or pemoline (if there are no contraindications, as described below, to their use).

It is important for parents to realize that the effects of stimulant drugs (with the possible exception of pemoline) last for only a brief period of time. For the amphetamines and methylphenidate there is no carryover and for pemoline there is generally no carryover from one day to the next. If the medication is effective, the parents will find that if the medication is discontinued for a day, the child's temperamental problems will promptly reappear. Thus, the child's HA problems may be present in the morning until he receives his medication. If part of his problem is dawdling about getting dressed, eating breakfast, and going to school, it may be useful or necessary to give him the medication as soon as he awakens. Similarly, the effect of the medicine will wear off as the day goes on. If the medicine wears off at three or four o'clock and a parent's main contacts with the child are only after he comes home from school, the parent may get the impression that the medicine is not helping. To check up on this, the parent should carefully observe the child's behavior on the weekend, at times when the medicine is most active, that is, mornings and early afternoons. Since the medicines are generally given in doses that permit the effects to wear off in the late afternoon or early evening, parents may anticipate more difficulty with the child at that time. If they are planning to take the child out in the evening or, say, to attend a large family gathering, it is often helpful to give a small additional dose later in the afternoon. As a rule this is not done routinely because, as will be mentioned below, these drugs tend to keep children awake.

As we mentioned, the physician will usually begin with the smallest dose of medication that has been found useful with HA children. He will then follow the principle of increasing the medication until either the child's behavioral problems improve to what seems to be the greatest possible extent, or the side effects of increased dosages cause a problem in themselves.

In order to determine how much benefit the child is receiving, the physician will want to know what is happening at home and what is happening at school. The schoolteacher is in an excellent position to determine the effects of medicine on the child. She sees him in a circumstance in which he is apt to have the most difficulty. Furthermore, she can compare his behavior with that of many other children of his age and intellectual ability. It is an excellent idea for the parent to stay in regular contact with the teacher whenever the medication is being adjusted or changed. The parent should tell the teacher that the child is receiving treatment and should ask for a report on any changes that the teacher may notice in the child's classroom behavior. Practically, it is useful not to make a big issue about this kind of information. Most people who expect to find changes tend to see them even if they are not present, so the parent should merely request information from the teacher and not suggest that she should expect to see the child improve. Another reason for not suggesting that the child may improve is that many teachers, trying to spare parents' feelings, will fail to report any difficulty the child may be having in school. If the child improves somewhat, and is now only a minor problem rather than a major problem, the teacher may inform the parent that things are going "pretty well." What the parent wants to know is if there are *any* problems, what kind they are, and how bad they are.

When the medicine is given depends on the sorts of problems the HA child has. If they occur primarily in school, many physicians will prescribe the medicine only during the school week and not on weekends, holidays, and vacations. If there are problems both at school and at home, the physician will recommend that the medication be given every day. After the medicine has been taken for some time most physicians like to employ "vacations from therapy" or medication-free periods. This is done for two reasons. The first is to give the child a rest from medicine. Although there is no evidence that these medications are harmful, most physicians would prefer to give as little as possible of any medicine. A second reason for giving rest periods is to see if the child has outgrown his need for the medication. Often, as the child grows older, he will need the medication only during his stressful periods. That means that the medication can be stopped during school vacations. As the child becomes still older, the physician may want the child to begin school in the fall without medication and see how he does through the first few weeks.

During this time the parents should, of course, stay in close touch with the school to see if problems are developing. If no problems emerge, that will provide considerable evidence that the HA child is outgrowing his problems. As discussed before, the parents should always bear in mind that hyperactivity and restlessness themselves may disappear, whereas other problems, such as poor concentration and underachievement, may persist. The parents should therefore request detailed information from the teacher. Information that the child is not restless is not sufficient. How he is adjusting with his classmates, how he is concentrating on his tasks, and how much work he is able to do and how well must all be examined closely.

A final point. Unlike adults, children generally do *not* become tolerant to the effects of these medications, although it is common to see a small amount of tolerance develop during the first few weeks of treatment. In those instances one finds that a dosage of medication that for a month or so provided relief of symptoms gradually fails to control those symptoms. The physician will then usually increase the medication and find no further development of tolerance. Usually, if a child stays on the medication for several years, he will require an increased dose of medication as he becomes older and larger. In a *few* instances children do become tolerant to one of the stimulant drugs. In such circumstances most physicians then switch to another of these drugs. Occasionally it is necessary to alternate drugs in this manner. If the development of a drug tolerance continues to present a problem, the physician will often then switch to still another of the major categories of medications that are used.

3. Side Effects

When given to children the stimulant drugs are unusually safe medications. Because the stimulants have opposite effects in children and adults (as noted, adults are made high and excited; children are not made high and are often made calm), the effect of these medications is sometimes called paradoxical. This is true only in some respects and not in others. In *both* children and adults the stimulant drugs decrease appetite and tend to interfere with sleep. Usually the child's appetite returns after a while. Occasionally the effect on appetite continues and is accompanied by some degree of weight loss. Although this weight loss may produce some concern in the parents, it never occurs to a medically serious degree. The drugs' tendency to keep some children awake can usually be controlled by careful administration. Medication keeps children awake only while it is still in the bloodstream (that is, 3 to 6 hours after the last dose of pills and up to 18 to 24 hours for the long-acting capsules). This is the reason for *not* giving these medications late in the day. If sleeplessness continues to be a problem, it can generally be handled by *not* using the long-acting form of the medicine but by using pills instead and by being careful not to give the last pill too late in the day. When the medication is adjusted this way, sleeplessness will not be a problem. However, behavior problems may appear later in the day as the medication wears off.

Allergies to the amphetamines and methylphenidate are very rare. Approximately 1 to 2 percent of children receiving pemoline will develop an allergy to the medicine. The allergy is not evident from symptoms such as skin rash but can be detected initially only by means of blood tests. Because some children do become allergic to pemoline and because it can only be detected in its early stages by blood tests, children receiving pemoline must have such blood tests every few months. In the event that allergy develops, pemoline must be discontinued. So far as we know, there are usually no long-term ill effects after its discontinuation.

4. Stimulant Medications and Growth

Several years ago a report was published stating that stimulant medications decreased the rate of growth of both height and weight in HA children. Since that report appeared, a number of other studies on the same subject have been published, some making the same claims and others stating that height was not affected by stimulant medication. Physicians are still unsure, and even the reports claiming that height was affected did not show very appreciable changes. For example, the child may have grown a quarter of an inch less than he was expected to in that year. As indicated, such findings are tentative. Furthermore, some physicians have suggested that HA children may have growth patterns that are different from those of other children, so that the usual tables of growth may not apply to HA children. Research is being conducted to determine the exact effects of stimulant medication on growth.

There is no doubt that many HA children do lose weight on stimulant medication. As we said, although this is sometimes upsetting to parents, there is no information suggesting that it is harmful, and apparently weight returns to normal when the medication is stopped. We should reemphasize that the effects that have been reported are small and that most physicians treating HA children regard the psychological benefits as outweighing *possible* effects on the rate of growth. Even if research does show that height is appreciably affected—and we repeat, that has as yet *not* been shown—parents will have to ask themselves whether they want their child to be tall and unhappy or somewhat shorter and better adjusted. At a practical level, what the physician must do is follow the child's height and weight and base the use of stimulant medication not only on its effect on growth but on its effects on the child's psychological well-being.

MAJOR TRANQUILIZERS

Another group of medications used in the treatment of hyperactivity consists of the so-called major tranquilizers. These medications, first discovered about thirty years ago, have been used in the treatment of serious psychiatric disorders in adults. They are sometimes used when the stimulant drugs are ineffective, and are sometimes extremely effective. They are absolutely nonhabit-forming or addicting, and with certain precautions are very safe. There are literally dozens of these medications, many of them very similar chemically. They are also very similar in their effects, with some slight differences that make now one, now another, desirable for an individual child. Those most generally employed, and this list is far from complete, are: chlorpromazine (Thorazine); thioridazine (Mellaril); trifluoperazine (Stelazine);

haloperidol (Haldol). Sometimes physicians will employ still other compounds if for some reason those most commonly used seem undesirable in a particular instance.

1. Effects

When these medications are effective, children gradually become less anxious, quieter, and easier to live with and to manage. The medications have two effects. At first they tend to produce sleepiness, but after several days or weeks, the sleepy (or groggy) feelings tend to disappear. The sleep-producing quality of the medicine is not what is being sought, but in order to obtain the useful tranquilizer effects one must put up with the sleepiness for a while.

2. Dosage

The doses of different tranquilizing medications vary considerably. For example, chlorpromazine is usually given in amounts ranging from about 30 to 600 milligrams a day. Haloperidol, which is more potent, may be given in doses ranging from .5 to 10 milligrams. As with the stimulant medications, it is impossible to predict how much medication a given child will require. Sometimes a very large, very active child may require a comparatively small dose, whereas a small and somewhat quieter child may require a larger dose. For this reason, as with stimulants, the physician will generally begin with a small dose, gradually increasing the amount until the problems seem to be well controlled. The parents should therefore expect that the doctor will frequently increase the dose at first, and they should not be upset because he does so. In order to simplify the giving of medication, tablets of different sizes are generally employed. The physician usually begins with the smallest dose tablet, to permit flexibility, and then if the dose is increased he substitutes larger tablets so that the child need not take a fistful of pills every day.

An important point about treatment with tranquilizers is that they are among the medications that sometimes require several weeks of administration before a maximum cumulative effect becomes apparent. Even after the correct dosage has been reached, full improvement may not be seen for several weeks.

The medicines *sometimes* act long enough so that they can occasionally be given in only one dose a day. In such cases, medication is usually given every night, approximately 1 or 2 hours before the child's bedtime. The sleep effect of the medication appears approximately an hour after the medicine is given and wears off after 4 to 6 hours. (As mentioned, during the first few days or weeks the sleepiness will be more marked.) If the medicine is given 1 or 2 hours before bedtime it will assure a good night's sleep and will not make the child very groggy in the morning. Usually the medicine does *not* appear to have a long-lasting effect and may have to be given two or three times a day.

3. Side Effects
As mentioned in the general discussion of medication, most medications can produce allergies, and this is the case with the major tranquilizers. Usually if allergies develop, they do so within the first few weeks or months that a new medicine is given. Since developing allergies can sometimes be detected in the earlier stages by their effects on the blood count, some physicians obtain a blood count before the child starts the medication and at intervals thereafter. If a child has received the medication for a long time and has not developed an allergy, the risk of his developing one later is much smaller. For this reason, as time goes on, the physician will obtain blood tests less frequently or discontinue them altogether.

Another annoying, but not dangerous, side effect is that some of these medications make children more susceptible to irritation by the sun. A few children who receive major tranquilizers and are exposed to the sun will develop an itchy rash. If this happens, the correct treatment is for the child to wear long-sleeved clothing and to be exposed to the sun as little as possible.

A third annoying side effect, *sometimes* seen if children require comparatively *large* doses of these medications, involves some degree of muscular stiffness, shaking, and trembling. These symptoms are not serious and are routinely handled by giving another medicine that controls them.

Still other allergic symptoms can occur with these medications, as with any other, but they are rare. To be absolutely safe, a parent should notify the doctor of any unusual symptoms.

Although these side effects do occur in some children, they are infrequent. It is necessary to be aware of them, but it is not necessary to be very concerned about them.

ANTIDEPRESSANTS

A third group of medications that have proved useful in some hyperactive children consists of drugs that are employed for the treatment of serious depressions in adults. These drugs, like the major tranquilizers, are *absolutely* non-habit-forming. If given to an adult who is not depressed or to a child who is not hyperactive, they make the person irritable and/or anxious. They certainly do not make him high. A normal adult or nonhyperactive child would find the effects of these medications unpleasant and would not want to continue to take them. The antidepressants are not used routinely now for two reasons. First, they appear to be not as effective as the stimulant medications. Second, as yet it is not known what effects they would have if used in the treatment of hyperactive children over a period of years. As the medical treatment of hyperactive children often requires that the medication be given daily for a number of years, physicians will need more experience with antidepressants given over a long period before prescribing them routinely.

As with the major tranquilizers, there are several antidepressants that are employed. The two most common are probably imipramine (Tofranil) and amitriptyline (Elavil).

1. Dosage

Most children require between 30 and 200 milligrams of these medications a day. Since susceptibility to the medicines varies widely from child to child, the physician will generally begin with a low dose and gradually increase it over a period of several weeks until either the child's symptoms improve or the side effects of the medicine become unpleasant. As with other medications, the parent must be prepared to wait several weeks before it can be determined whether these medications will prove effective. There are slight differences between imipramine and amitriptyline, as well as the other medications, and sometimes a child may respond better to one than another. Since there is no way of predicting the child's responsiveness, the physician will often have to try several of these agents before reaching the best one.

As with the major tranquilizers, these medications sometimes produce some sleepiness the first few weeks they are administered. The sleepiness generally goes away with the passage of time. Generally the physician will have to wait until the child has developed a tolerance to the sleepiness before increasing the dose of the medication.

2. Side Effects

In addition to sleepiness, antidepressants sometimes produce other unpleasant nondangerous side effects, such as irritability, dry mouth, mild constipation, and mild dizziness. Generally the side effects diminish with the passage of time or can be controlled by lowering the dose slightly. These medications rarely produce allergy, but as a precautionary measure periodic blood tests may be made to determine if one is developing.

OTHER MEDICATIONS

There are many other medications that sometimes prove effective when the substances listed above do not. In rare instances a physician may have to try as many as six or eight, and the parents may have to wait several months before finding out if there is a medication that will benefit the child.

Recently a few physicians have suggested the use of very large doses of vitamins in the treatment of children and adults with psychological difficulties; mega-vitamin therapy has been described as a safe and effective treatment for several kinds of behavioral disorders. At present all one can say is that these claims are unsubstantiated. Nevertheless, the parent might believe that a trial use of large doses of vitamins would at least be natural and therefore safe. The difficulty is that although the vitamins are natural, doses of ten to a thousand times the normal daily requirement are not natural and may not be safe. Salt and water are natural but someone who drinks many times the normal requirement of water in a day might well die of water intoxication. Although further information may show vitamin therapy to be effective and safe, there is now no evidence affirming that it is effective, and more evidence is needed to show that it is safe.

As can be seen from the above discussion, no medication used in the treatment of HA children is ideal. Each medication has some, usually minor, disadvantages. Perhaps in the future more convenient, safer, and more effective medications will be developed. In the meantime the medications available are usually effective (often dramatically so) and safe, and in the large majority of instances their advantages completely outweigh their disadvantages.

AIDS TO ADMINISTERING MEDICATION

Many parents do not realize it, but there are important psychological aspects to giving and taking medication. This is overlooked because most medications most people take are either for medical conditions or for obvious psychological ones. People take aspirin because of a headache, laxatives because of constipation, and tranquilizers because of anxiety. The hows and whys are straightforward. But in the administration of medicine to children for hyperactivity, several psychological principles play an important role. If treatment is to be maximally effective, these principles must be properly applied.

First, the child must have some understanding of why he is receiving medication. Second, he must be assured that taking medicine does not mean that his problems are terrible, such as being brain-damaged or crazy. Third, it is useful to have him recognize and acknowledge problems in his own behavior *that he himself does not like,* so that he will not feel that medicine is being given to him simply so that other people can tolerate him more. If a child does not understand why he is receiving medication, if he does not feel that he has problems and that the medicine is helping him with these problems, he is likely to resist taking it, to forget taking it, or to discontinue taking it when he grows older but may still need it.

Usually an HA child will recognize and acknowledge certain features of his experience and behavior that he does not like or that get him into trouble that he does not like. These may include such things as not being able to pay attention, having a hot temper, being "nervous" (restless), or being criticized by teachers or parents for forgetting things, not finishing work, or being out of the classroom seat all the time. He can honestly be told that the medicine will *help* him to complete his schoolwork, to pay attention, to hold his temper, to be less nervous, to remember things better, and to calm down. If he can accept the fact that the medicine is helping *him,* a large task has been accomplished. He will feel that something is being done *for* him rather than to him.

It is also important in giving medicine to children that they do not get the idea that because they have to take medicine they are somehow excused from assuming responsibility for their own behavior. HA, like any other illness, does not negate free will. It may limit or modify someone's behavioral options, but it does not eliminate them. Children *can and must feel* that they share a responsibility for their behavior. They should not attribute all their actions to powers beyond their control. They should not be allowed to play the kind of "game" that Eric Berne, in his book *Games People Play,* calls "wooden leg." In this psychological "game," the person says the equivalent of "What can you expect of me? I couldn't do more. I've got a wooden leg." Children should be prevented from adopting the same attitude with regard to their HA. They should not be allowed to imply: "I am a psychological cripple. I have HA. All my actions are beyond my own control." For this reason, parents (and this applies to teachers and brothers and sisters as well) should not explain the HA child's behavior on the basis of whether or not he's taken his medication. Parents should not say to him: "You are acting up. When did you have your medicine?" Putting things this way leads the child to believe that he has no control of himself, and it may put him in the position of having his "badness" explained by the absence of medicine and his "goodness" explained by its presence. If so, he can take no credit for controlling himself, and when he has not behaved in an appropriate way, he frequently can excuse himself because he hasn't taken his medication. If in talking to the HA child, his parents, teachers, or brothers and sisters often associate his behavior with his medication schedule, he soon will learn how to play the game of "medicine wooden leg": "What can you expect of me? I am HA and my medicine has worn off."

The importance of communicating to children their responsibility for their own behavior will become clearer in the major section of this chapter entitled "Psychological Management."

DIETARY TREATMENT

As we mentioned earlier, some physicians have suggested that HA may be due to bodily reactions to normal food constituents. One possibility is that some children may be allergic to certain foods and the allergy may produce behavioral problems. (See chapter 3 page 25.) A second, and different, claim has been made by a California physician, Dr. Ben Feingold (*Why Your Child is Hyperactive,* Random House, 1975), who claims that many children become HA as a reaction to artificial colorings, flavorings, some preservatives (which may be present in processed foods) and salicylates (a chemical related to aspirin) that are found naturally in some fruits and vegetables. A diet that eliminates these chemicals is called a food-additive-free or Feingold diet. The idea that food additives might cause HA is particularly appealing to those people who believe that food additives are "unnatural" (and therefore probably harmful) and because treatment with a special, healthful diet seems preferable to treatment with drugs. When children are put on these special diets without any attempt to disguise the treatment, some children do seem to show significant change in behavior. This is probably due to the change in the family's attitude about that child (which usually means more time spent with that child) and hopeful expectations in the minds of the child and his family. However, all the carefully conducted, controlled studies—in which the family does not know whether or not the child is on the additive-free diet—have shown that one type of additives (the artificial food colorings) does not produce significant hyperactivity (though it may produce some minor changes in attention in some children). Because there is still some room to hope that the food-additive-free diet may help *some* children, there would be no harm in families' trying this special diet as long as they pay attention to good nutrition and remain particularly alert to the need for vitamin C. (The Feingold diet limits the intake of several popular vitamin-C-containing fruits.) So far, however, we remain pessimistic about any relationship between food additives and HA.

The subject of food allergies remains controversial. Some physicians believe that food allergies are frequently the cause of behavioral problems, while many others either doubt the existence of food allergies or think they occur infrequently and usually only in infants and toddlers. Doctors argue about this issue because there are no laboratory tests that can diagnose whether a food allergy exists. Therefore, the diagnosis must be made on the basis of clinical judgment—which means there is room for disagreement. Most physicians agree that the only certain way to diagnose food allergies is through an elimination diet. This usually means removing all but the most basic, simple foods from the child's diet and then gradually, one at a time, adding foods back and observing the child's reaction. This is a tedious and time-consuming process that requires much patience on the part of both child and parent. For that reason, there has to be fairly good evidence that allergy may be a problem before most physicians are willing to try the elimination diet. It is our impression, as mentioned previously (see chapter 3 page 26), that the symptoms of food allergy are really different from the symptoms of true HA. It may be that an occasional HA child *may* show improvement if he is found to be allergic to certain foods and is placed on a diet which does not contain them. If parents think that food allergies may be causing problems for their child, it is probably a good idea for them to seek a physician's help in identifying possible allergies and then placing the child on a special diet that does not include the targeted foods. Although some pediatricians will investigate a child's possible food allergies, many would prefer that the child be seen by a pediatric allergist. It is important for the parents to realize, however, that at present there is little evidence that food allergies play any substantial role in the behavior problems associated with hyperactivity.

Coffee

A few years ago someone proposed that HA might be less common in South American countries—which may or may not be true—because children there drank coffee. As coffee contains caffeine, a recognized stimulant of the brain, and, because stimulants seem to help HA, it was inferred that caffeine might be useful in treating HA. A few studies have been conducted and they seem to indicate that caffeine, by itself, is *not* useful in treating HA. When caffeine is combined with stimulant drug treatment, the overall response is better than with stimulant drugs alone, but the same good response can be obtained simply by increasing the amount of the stimulant drug. Because caffeine is less effective than the stimulant medication and has a variety of side effects that are considered undesirable, coffee does not have a useful place in the treatment of the HA child.

Psychological Management

Most HA children can benefit from medication. All HA children can benefit from understanding and correct handling. HA children have special problems but like all other children they may have "unspecial" problems as well. Difficulties, misunderstandings, friction between parent and child, will cause trouble for any child. They may cause more trouble for the HA child. This book focuses on the particular psychological problems the HA child is likely to develop because he is hyperactive.

UNDERSTANDING THE PROBLEM

The first part of this book has been devoted to a description of the typical problems of the HA child and *why* he has these problems. The "why" is very important. It is very difficult to understand that a child who is attention-demanding, contrary, and short-tempered may be having a "physical" problem. Intuitively, one believes that he is having a "psychological" problem. As has been said, he does have psychological problems but they are physically caused.

If this is so, how should the parent handle the problems? It *seems* that if a problem is "psychological" the child is "responsible" for his behavior. If he is good he should be praised and if he is bad he should be punished. Similarly, if the problem is "physical," the child is not "responsible" for his behavior. If that is so, he should *not* be rewarded for being good or be punished for being bad. Neither of the above beliefs is true. Temperament may influence behavior but is not the only factor that determines behavior. Temperament may make it easier or harder for a child to control himself. It may make it easier for him to learn to respond to discipline. But how the parents feel about the child and how they treat him can have appreciable effects.

During the past few years psychiatrists and psychologists have found that patients whose severe psychological problems are physically caused can be benefited markedly by psychological treatment. Mongolism, a severe form of retardation, is physically caused, but certain techniques of training can teach children with this disorder more effectively. Psychosis, severe psychological disturbances in adults, may produce childlike, withdrawn, or destructive behavior. These patients, whose symptoms are worse than those of any HA child, can in many cases be helped by certain techniques. These techniques are based on three principles: (1) making the patients responsible for their behavior; (2) rewarding them for good behavior; (3) punishing them (in a special way) for bad behavior.

Similarly, the HA child does better when he is held accountable, made responsible, for his behavior. He should not be allowed to say, either in so many words or indirectly, "I'm hyperactive— I'm a mental cripple—I'm not responsible for what I do." He should be treated as responsible, and if necessary he should be told something to this effect: "You do have problems that may sometimes make it hard for you to control yourself. But the same thing is true for everybody. Everyone does some things more easily than others and does other things with more difficulty. You can learn to [count to ten, hold your temper, not tease your sister] and I expect you to." As with all our suggestions, of course, the parents should change the words to suit themselves and their children.

In other words, the child should not be held to be either irresponsible or blameworthy. He should be treated as someone who has a greater tendency than average to do certain things. On the other hand, the parents should realize that for most HA children no method of child rearing will eliminate certain tendencies. The child *will* tend to be more attention-seeking and forgetful, and will seem absentminded and willful. In most instances he is not doing these things to annoy. He would do them no matter how he had been raised. This distinction between symptoms that can be benefited by both rearing and medicine and those that can be alleviated only by medicine is important to remember. It will prevent the parent from trying to use psychological methods to change things that cannot be changed (or at best changed *very* little) in this way. Although psychologically unchangeable symptoms vary from child to child, they usually include the following: short attention span, distractibility, moodiness, lack of stick-to-itiveness, school underachievement, and immaturity. They *may* include bed-wetting, soiling, and some antisocial behaviors such as stealing. Again remember that although psychological techniques may not completely eliminate these problems in the child, they may help the child. For example, the child may continue to have tantrums, but he can be taught what to do when he has them. This will be discussed later.

In summary, there are three things for the parent to remember. One, the child does have difficulties in doing and not doing certain things. Two, he will learn best how to compensate for his problems if he is treated as a responsible person who can gradually learn to control himself and his behavior. Three, the degree to which his problems can be helped by particular child-rearing techniques varies. It is much easier to teach him how to control his temper or how to take responsibility for his chores than to teach him to have a longer attention span or to be less distractible. The first kind of problem (for example, temper, chores) will be helped by both medicine and discipline. The second kind of problem (for example, short attention span) for the most part can be helped only by medicine.

BASIC PROCEDURES

The main problem of the HA child at home, as we have stated several times, involves discipline. In discussing the basic procedures that will help the child to function effectively in his home environment, we shall first indicate how the parents can establish constructive rules for the child. The second section will describe the rewards and punishments that are most likely to ensure that the child will adhere to the rules.

1. Establishing Rules

There is considerable evidence that certain ways of handling HA children are more effective than others. It has been found that a firm, consistent, explicit, predictable home environment is the best. We shall elaborate the special meaning that these terms have with respect to disciplining the HA child. *Firm* means that rules and/or expectations for the child *always* have the same consequences. If he breaks a particular rule he is always punished and always in the same way. If he does what he is asked he *always* obtains acknowledgment and/or praise. *Consistent* means that the rules themselves do not change from day to day. If he is supposed to clean up his room before going out to play he is *never* allowed to leave his room until it has been cleaned up. *Explicit* means clearly defined and clearly understood by all parties. For example, *cleaned up* could mean that clothes have been hung in the closet, or that the bed has been made, or that toys have been returned to a shelf, or that the room has been vacuumed and dusted, or any combination of these things. For the cleaning-up rule, the definition of *cleaning up* must be explicit enough so that the child and the parents understand the rule the same way. *Predictable* means that laws are made before, not after the crime. Obviously all the parental expectations for the child cannot be stated beforehand. Parents never consider telling the toddler not to put nail polish on the rug and never consider telling him not to put a toy car in his ear. Some things can be dealt with only after they happen. In general, however, for most daily activities, rules can and should be made and then enforced. The child must wash himself, brush his teeth, do his around-the-house chores, and do his homework every day; rules concerning these routine functions should be established. Punishment should follow any violation of the rules, but should not be employed if the rules have not been agreed upon beforehand. Analogous consistent and predictable rules for adults exist in the speed limits for driving. It is easier to abide by a specific speed limit, say, 55 mph, than adhere to the vague limit, "reasonable and proper," that was formerly designated in some Western states. In the case of the vague speed limit one does not know how fast he can go if it is twilight and a light rain is falling. Someone who is fearful may drive 35 mph. Someone who is more adventurous and drives at 40 mph may rightly be upset when he gets a ticket.

The above suggestions may impress parents as harsh and possibly cruel. They may also seem to contradict various benign permissive doctrines that advocate allowing children to "do their own thing," and allow opportunities for parents and children to talk things over. Let us correct some common misconceptions. First, *firmness* is not the same as harshness. Harshness is excessively severe or brutal rule enforcement. It is harsh to imprison someone for life for driving too fast. It is firm to *always* fine him. Second, children need structure. They need established rules, expectations, and values by which to live. Such structure does not mean the absence of freedom.

All people living in society have to follow certain rules and expectations if that society is to function effectively. Adults must not steal, drive when drunk, or embezzle. They must not urinate in public. Behaving in accordance with such rules also benefits the individual. First, and obviously, it keeps him out of trouble. But it also helps some individuals directly. Someone who has only poorly learned to control his impulses must consume a large part of his energy in simply controlling himself. The reformed alcoholic or dope addict must expend a great deal of effort in preventing himself from backsliding. The person who has learned to control himself readily has energies that he can utilize profitably elsewhere.

Note that this is not contrary to self-expression or creativity. The person who can handle his energies can create. The person who cannot channel his energies may be brilliant but he will not be productive (consider the old saw that genius is 1 percent inspiration and 99 percent perspiration). Firm, consistent rules for behavior have nothing at all to do with the child's self-expression, nor understanding between parent and child. We have been talking about rules for behavior, not rules for thoughts and feelings. Thoughts and feelings are *very* different from behavior. Thoughts and feelings cannot be regulated and the parent should *not* attempt to regulate them. As will be discussed later, parents should help their child acknowledge and express his feelings. But both the parent and the child should always discriminate between feelings and behavior. For example, the parents of a hyperactive child should allow him to express his jealous feelings toward his newborn sister, but he should not be allowed to hit her. Feeling jealous and hitting because of jealousy should be recognized as being as different as night and day.

Finally, the setting of firm rules need not interfere with helpful discussions between the parents and the child. As the child becomes older such discussions certainly should be a part of family life, but even when he is younger, they may be helpful. The child may, for example, suggest ways of getting his tasks done in a way that *he* likes better and that does not compromise the family. This is perfectly acceptable and in fact should be encouraged.* But talking things over should not prevent rules from being formulated. It may influence how they are decided upon and it may modify their exact terms but it should not interfere with their being established explicitly and consistently.

What evidence is there that the kind of structure discussed here is useful? Very interesting information comes from a study done

---

*For an excellent discussion of this issue, the parent can very profitably consult Thomas Gordon's *Parent Effectiveness Training*. New York: Peter H. Wyden [McKay], 1970.

in the middle thirties with severely HA children. The behavior of these children was so uncontrollable at home that they had to be placed in a hospital for children with this serious behavior problem. The physicians had no previous experience with such HA children and tried various techniques to see which would be most effective. They began by assuming that the problems of these children were the result of excessive emotional stress and strain and treated the children with a great deal of tolerance. This technique produced a brief period of improvement, which was soon followed by a recurrence of the same behavioral problems. Next, since the children had never received psychotherapy, they were treated in individual psychotherapy. This approach, too, proved unsuccessful. Finally, the doctors decided to employ an environment that was "constructive," "restrictive," and "tolerant." The rules were not lax, and definite compliance to them was expected of the children. Children were isolated but not criticized for impulsive behavior (we shall discuss this isolation later), and after they had calmed down they were helped to express themselves. This last technique clearly produced the greatest benefit, and many children could be discharged from the hospital to their homes. Unfortunately, those children who returned to homes where the parents could not be firm often again became disturbed and had to return to the hospital. It is important to emphasize that not all children were benefited by this (or any other) technique, but this was the technique that worked *best*.

There is reason to believe, therefore, that these techniques of rearing can help HA children. There is also reason to believe that they are most effective if begun early in life and that they are relatively ineffective (perhaps useless) if begun very late in childhood. The techniques to be discussed may help the preschool or young school-age child a great deal. They may be totally ineffective with a hyperactive child who is approaching adolescence.

What the specific rules should be in a particular family depends on parental preference and the age of the child. Parents could theoretically make any rules and teach *young* children to abide by them. (Different cultures have vastly different rules and standards for child behavior, and each culture succeeds in making a "standard product," a child well adapted to living in that culture.) As the child grows older, the parents' latitude decreases. The young child is for the most part only aware of how his own family does things. The older child is very much aware of how other children and their families do things, and will tend to rebel if his parents' standards appear to be different. A mother may keep her two-year-old boy in long curls and he will not know enough to protest. But it would be foolish of her to try to keep her fourteen-year-old in a crewcut when his friends look like George Washington. The earlier that rules and values are taught to a child the more likely he will be to maintain them later, even in the face of different standards outside the family.

To repeat, the techniques to be discussed work *best* on younger children, say, up to the age of ten or eleven. These methods, which require that the child still be dependent on and controlled by his parents, are *not* for teen-agers. Teen-agers require a different psychological approach.

With younger children, the first task for the parents is to decide, concretely and specifically, what behaviors of the child require limitations or change. It is important to be concrete and specific so that the rules can be stated clearly and explicitly, as discussed earlier. Let us give some instances of vague, meaningless rules and how they may be clarified.

A. "He should clean his room." As we have already indicated, this is a highly ambiguous rule. If by "cleaning the room" the parent mean "put everything away," and the child understands "make your bed," he can feel wronged if he makes his bed, leaves, and is criticized. Furthermore, there is room for endless debate. The child cleaned the room by *his* standards but he did not clean the room by his mother's standards. We shall return to this particular topic in a later subsection entitled "Chores."

B. "He should have better table manners." This might mean: he should eat with his fork instead of his fingers; he should put a napkin on his lap; he should say "please," or he should not use a boardinghouse reach, etc.

C. "He should treat his little sister better." This might mean: he should not hit her; he should allow her to play with his toys; he should not retaliate if she hits him, etc.

D. "He should be neater." This might mean: he should tie his shoelaces; button his shirt, wash his face, brush his teeth.

Not only does the child not know what the parents mean if they are not specific—and he can and will argue with them in the best legalistic fashion about what they might have meant—but also parents will have a much harder time knowing if progress has really taken place.

The second task of the parents is to establish a hierarchy of importance of rules. They must decide what is essential, what is important, what would be nice, and what is trivial. The parents must decide what are five-star rules and what are one-star rules. They must fit the punishment to the crime; they must distinguish between felonies and misdemeanors. They must not, so to speak, punish illegal parking with life imprisonment and punish murder with a warning. For example, parents have been known to use a talk as punishment for the setting of a serious fire, and a severe spanking as punishment for poor homework. The usefulness of establishing five- and one-star rules is that it helps the parents to concentrate on the more important areas first and gives the child some breathing room. After the most essential problems have been brought under control, the parents can move to the next category.

Another task for the parents is to predecide that both shall abide by the prescribed course of action. This policy is not always easy to carry out. As has been discussed earlier, frequently each parent has devised his or her own (usually not too successful) technique for dealing with the child, and, unfortunately, it is equally common for each to believe that that technique is right and the child's problems are the result of the other's mismanagement. If such a family atmosphere exists, it conflicts with the consistent united front that is an absolute requirement for helping the HA child learn to control his behavior. It is not necessary that the parents agree completely with each other. It is necessary only that they act in common. If the parents are incapable of resolving their differences and agreeing upon rules and standards for their HA child's behavior, they may benefit from psychological assistance. A psychiatrist, social worker, or psychologist may enable them to thrash out their differences and decide upon the set of rules, and the relative importance of the various rules necessary for the HA child.

2. Rewards and Punishments

In addition to establishing sound rules to help the child, the parents must predecide on a plan of rewards and punishments. The rewards and punishments should be seen as such by the child and not only by the parents. The words *reward* and *punishment* have an unfortunate meaning to some people. Reward seems to suggest bribery and punishment seems to suggest brutality. All that is meant by reward is something the child likes, particularly attention, praise, or a small special privilege. Certain privileges, toys, and so forth can be useful under special conditions, which will be discussed later.

Similarly, punishment simply means something the child does not like. It does not mean beating, or depriving of privileges for a long time. Generally, with younger children, a most effective and nonhurtful punishment is sending the child to his room until he stops behaving in an undesirable way (for example, having a tantrum) or finishes a required task (for example, getting dressed). It is more effective to say, "Go to your room, please, and come back to breakfast when your shoes are tied and your face is washed," than it is to yell at the child and/or beat him. We shall return to the question of superior kinds of rewards and punishments shortly.

There are two more very important principles of reward and punishment. First, to be most useful, a reward or punishment should be immediate. Any delay decreases effectiveness. When a child does what you want him to, praise him on the spot. If he does what he has been told not to do, punish him at once. Do not offer distant presents ("any toy you want two weeks from now") or threaten punishment ("Daddy will spank you when he gets home"). Second, the one-time rule should be adopted. The parents should learn the habit of saying *do* or *don't* only *once* before rewarding or punishing. If they do not apply this rule, if they give first, second, third, and tenth warnings before acting, their children will learn to commit ten violations before worrying. In the meantime the parents will have developed a sore throat and built up a good head of angry steam. In some cases, the child may have been anxiously pushing his parent to take a stand. Surprisingly, most children are relieved when the parent finally acts. A good deal of friction can be avoided by the use of this one-time rule.

In the past thirty years, psychologists have learned a great deal about reward and punishment from animal experimentation. Researchers have discovered extremely simple and effective techniques that can be used to teach lower animals, such as pigeons and rats, to perform very complicated tasks. For example, it is fairly easy to teach a rat to push a bar for food when a certain colored light is on and to push another bar to avoid receiving a shock when another light is on. Using these techniques one may teach a rat to push a bar very slowly for food under one set of conditions and very rapidly for food under another set of conditions.

In the past twenty years or so, psychologists have found that such techniques are sometimes helpful in teaching and controlling the behavior of human beings whose psychological difficulties are so great that previously they seemed unreachable by any known technique—for example, profoundly retarded children and adults, children who are unable to talk despite the presence of normal intelligence, and seriously disturbed adult psychiatric patients. In more recent years a number of psychologists have tried applying these "operant" techniques to children with behavioral problems. The operant techniques—or operant conditioning—are no more than refined sets of rewards and punishments, and the work of the psychologists can be translated into recommendations that can be very helpful to parents of HA children.

The exact rules and laws of operant conditioning as they are used in the laboratory are somewhat complicated, but the basic principle that parents can make use of is exceedingly simple. The basic principle is that *acts are influenced by their consequences.* That is, what happens after an animal or child does something greatly influences, either positively or negatively, the likelihood of his doing the same thing again. For the parents, this means that how they act when their child does or says something will either increase or decrease the probability that the child will behave that way again.

This principle is most easy to illustrate in the use of operant conditioning with animals. In a typical experiment a hungry rat is placed in a simple cage with a bar in it. In the course of his explorations the rat eventually leans on the bar. When he does so a pellet of food is released automatically into the feeding dish. If one observes the rat through a one-way screen one sees that the rat may not return to the bar for a while. Eventually, perhaps by accident, he will depress the bar again, and again will be rewarded by food. As one continues to watch the rat, one finds that he eventually seems to "get the idea." After a day or two of training in such a cage the hungry rat will immediately go to the bar and press it. Notice that we use the phrase *get the idea*. Obviously we have no information about the consciousness of rats, and the phrase may be somewhat misleading, but in humans such behavior can be learned without awareness: some experiments seem to indicate the subjects may learn to change some kinds of behavior with no awareness whatsoever of the sequence that produces the change. That is, people may develop habits that produce certain consequences for them without being aware of any relationship between the habits, the acts based on those habits, and the consequences of those acts.

To illustrate the principle in animal experimentation again, let us discuss a typical demonstration in an elementary psychology course. A hungry pigeon is placed in a cage. Standing outside the cage and observing the pigeon through a one-way screen is the experimenter. In his hand he holds a switch with which he can cause a click to be made in the box and a kernel of corn to be delivered to the pigeon in a feeding dish. The experimenter may choose to make the pigeon perform any behavior of which pigeons are capable. In one instance it was decided to make the pigeon rotate counterclockwise, spinning like a ballerina. In order to accomplish this, the experimenter waited until the pigeon in his normal wanderings had turned slightly to the left. After the pigeon had done so, the experimenter pressed the switch and the pigeon received a kernel of corn. In the next 20 or 30 seconds the pigeon again turned to the left, and the experimenter delivered another kernel of corn. In the following few minutes the pigeon began to rotate slowly toward his left. After he had done so for a while the experimenter again delivered a kernel of corn. During the next 5 or 10 minutes the pigeon began to turn continuously in a circle. The experimenter would wait until the pigeon was turning rapidly and then, and only then, deliver the food. Thereafter when the pigeon turned slowly he received no food and when he turned rapidly he received the food. At the end of the half hour the class was astonished to see a pigeon rotating like a whirling dervish. This experiment illustrates the complex tasks that can be taught even to lower animals. More complex behavior can be taught to humans, and (as cannot be illustrated by animal experiments) such learning can apparently occur without the person's being aware or conscious of it as well as with his being conscious of it.

Before examining the question of what relevance these experiments have for people, let us digress for just a moment and define two, and only two, terms from operant conditioning therapy. The first term is *operant,* and the second term is *reinforcement.* An operant is any voluntary act an animal or human being is capable of performing. It includes the rat's bar-pressing, and the pigeon's circling. In fact, it includes most behavior. In children it might even include talking, attention-getting, having tantrums, waking up in the middle of the night, lying, stealing, crying, fire-setting, writing poems, or philosophizing—in short, almost anything. Reinforcement is synonymous with the word "reward." In the animal experiments discussed, "reinforcement" was food. Food is rewarding or reinforcing to a hungry animal.

What is reinforcing to children? That depends on their state. To the rat who has eaten his fill, food is no longer reinforcing, and he will not depress a bar to obtain it. In working with very disturbed psychiatric patients, therapists have occasionally used food as a reinforcer; such a procedure can sometimes be effective if the patients are kept somewhat hungry. Similarly, for a thirsty child, water can be reinforcing; for a hungry child, food can be reinforcing. However, most of the child's acts are influenced by parental behavior that is quite different from simple satisfaction of hunger or thirst. For an individual child, reinforcing behavior varies, *but there are certain parental acts and behaviors that are reinforcing to almost all children.* The most important, as we have suggested, are parental affection and parental attention. Parental attention is probably the single most common reinforcer in a child's daily life. It is important not only because of the frequency with which it is focused on the child, but also because it is reinforcing no matter what elicits it. Some kinds of punishment, therefore, are more rewarding to a child than ignoring him. Expressing disapproval of a child's most recent misdeed is giving him attention. Thus, paradoxically, the likelihood that a child will repeat a misdeed may be increased when the parent discusses the misdeed with the child at too great a length.

What about more severe punishment? The reinforcers we have discussed are referred to by psychologists as "positive reinforcers." What the layman refers to as punishment, the psychologist calls "negative reinforcement." Certain general principles have been learned about the effects and effectiveness of negative reinforcement.

To begin with, negative reinforcement *generally* reduces the likelihood of the repetition of the act that preceded it. Thus, as generations of parents have learned, with most children most of the time a good spanking is a pretty effective way of preventing a child from doing again what he just did that the parents didn't like. The rat who received a powerful electric shock after pressing the bar will refrain from doing so in the future or, at least, in the very near future. Psychologists have also learned some less obvious things about punishment. If it is very severe (for example, a very painful electric shock, which is almost enough to paralyze the animal), the animal is likely *never* to repeat the act again, but punishments of this nature are also likely to be accompanied by side effects that change the animal in a number of undesirable ways. Animals that receive such powerful punishment are apt to become erratic and often show disturbed ("neurotic") behavior in other areas. In experiments in which electric shocks have been used to teach dogs to avoid things, the dogs have become vicious, excited, withdrawn, or very fearful. In other words, punishment that is effective enough to prevent of-

fensive behavior permanently may produce more disturbing behavior than that which it prevented.

If, then, some punishment focuses attention on the child and
therefore reinforces poor behavior, and if severe punishment is
likely to produce bad side effects, the question arises as to
whether any forms of punishment can be reasonably effective.
Although psychologists disagree, it seems that there are lesser
degrees of punishment that can suppress behavior but only *temporarily*. That is, shocks that will not make the animal neurotic
are not likely to be effective for very long. The relevance of this
for children should be fairly obvious. Humane parents use only
moderate punishment, and in HA children, who are often not
particularly responsive to punishment, the effects of punishment
should not be expected to be long-lasting. And in fact they rarely
are.

Positive reinforcement, on the other hand, may not be permanent either, but with certain modifications may be extremely
long-lasting. Its virtue is that once the child is started on the right
track he is likely to receive reinforcement from people outside
the family. The child who is taught to be reasonably polite, mod-
erately obedient, and reasonably nonaggressive will be reinforced
by favorable attention from others, by making friends and suc-
ceeding.

There is one other feature of positive reinforcement that increases the possibility that it may have very long-lasting effects.
This aspect can also be illustrated by animal experimentation.
When a rat is trained to push a bar, he receives food on every bar
press. If one stops delivering a pellet each time the rat presses
the bar, after a while the rat pushes less and less frequently and
eventually stops. However, with a simple modification of the
experiment, the rat can be made to work a much longer time for
fewer pellets. Let us suppose we arrange the machine so that at
first the rat receives a pellet only on every second bar push. Then
after a while we arrange it so that he receives a pellet on every
third, and every fourth, and so on. Now suppose we tinker
around with the machinery (and this is very simple) so that the
rat is playing a slot machine, that is, he receives a pellet, *on the
average,* on every 20th or 50th or 100th bar press. Sometimes he

receives three pellets in a row. Sometimes he may have to press the bar 200 times before receiving a pellet. After a rat has been exposed to this payoff system he is very resistant to losing his habit. Again the relevance of this to children should be obvious. One begins by reinforcing the child every time he performs a desired behavior. After a while one changes the payoff and gradually reinforces him less for the same behavior. Like the rat in whom reinforcement has been tapered off in the same way, the child is now likely to persist in this behavior even without a constant payoff.

Having knocked punishment (and not for humane grounds but for practical grounds), we must back down a little and point out that it does have some effectiveness and that it can be important in situations that are dangerous or life-threatening. The two-year-old rushing out into the street (to possible death) should be punished fairly severely and immediately. This will decrease the likelihood of his doing it again in the near future. One is more likely to keep him out of the street, however, if he is positively reinforced for doing things that prevent his going there (for example, staying on the lawn or playing in the backyard). As we said earlier, punishment is a good temporary technique but it is ineffective in the long run in most HA children.

One point that we have touched upon but which bears repeating is the question of *when* reinforcement should occur. As we have said before, one word will suffice to answer this question. *Immediately*. In the experiments with animals, the success of the technique depends upon the animal's receiving the reinforcement the moment after the act—the operant—is performed. A delay of one second decreases its effectiveness a little, a delay of five seconds reduces it considerably, a delay of a minute makes it useless. Children apparently can tolerate longer delays but the same principle applies to them. Positive reinforcement (or reward) and negative reinforcement (or punishment) are *much more* effective if they are received immediately. If a child does what the parent wants him to do he should receive praise for that act immediately. If he does something that requires punishment, he should be punished immediately. As we have already indicated, it is ineffective and a waste of time to promise to reward the child in two weeks if he obtains good grades now or to delay necessary punishment until Daddy comes home. Such reinforcements *may* work at best temporarily (two weeks, or the rest of the day) but will have no long-lasting effect.

From this discussion the question emerges of how these techniques should be applied practically to children. They may be used informally and formally. Clearly, as indicated above, an important principle of their informal application is that children should be positively reinforced, immediately, when they do what their parents want. Once the child knows what his parents' desires are (for example, putting his shoes away, eating with a fork, saying "please"), he should be reinforced by his parents in a specific way whenever he performs these acts. By specific we mean that the parents should comment on the desired behavior in believable and pertinent terms. If he is asked to put his shoes away and does so, the parent should not say, "You are a wonderful son"; he or she should say, "I am very pleased that you are learning to take care of your things like a grown-up boy," or words to that effect. Children, like adults, recognize overgeneral praise as false. The child should know what he is receiving praise for.

Theoretically, the corresponding principle to be applied when children behave undesirably would require that the children be ignored, but how can the parent ignore undesirable behavior? If the child is acting like a clown it is easy. If he is pummeling his three-year-old sister or destroying the house, ignoring him is dangerous and/or expensive. If he is engaging in harmless attention-seeking behavior, ignoring is easy. If he is engaged in behavior that is destructive or harmful, ignoring should be combined with the isolation-room technique.

The usefulness of the isolation room becomes apparent when one considers what ordinarily happens when a child misbehaves. For example, if the child punches his sister, the parent is apt to ask at least, "Why did you do that?" Thus, the child receives *attention* for misbehaving. In accordance with the principles discussed, attention is likely to increase the probability that the child will do the same thing again. In other words, the parents' normal discussion with the child is likely to result in greater future misbehavior. With the isolation-room technique, the child is informed beforehand that whenever he misbehaves he will be sent to his room. Then when he actually does misbehave he is simply told that he is going to his room and that he will be allowed to come out as soon as he regains control of himself. If he goes willingly, that is fine. If he has to be carried, that may not be fine but it is effective. If he tries to leave his room, then a screen-door latch should be placed on the outside and locked.* When the child quiets down—or, in the case of the older child, when he announces that he has quieted down and comes out himself— then, and only then, does the parent sit down with the child and discuss what was bothering him before. With this technique the child receives attention for being in control of himself, not for being out of control. After a child has had considerable experience with this procedure, he often learns to go to his room when he has become upset and to come out when he is no longer upset. If the child has to be kept in the room, the parents should not let him out until he is able to be in control of himself, that is, until his tantrum has stopped or his anger outburst is under control. This technique has been used effectively with very disturbed hospitalized psychiatric patients as well as with hyperactive children. It is an especially effective technique with young (under the age of nine or ten) HA children.

The second way in which reinforcement therapy can be applied, the more formal way, cannot be used with the youngest HA children, but is effective with children beyond, say, the age of six. With this method the parent and the child decide what tasks the parents would like the child to perform. These may be tasks that occur every day or once a week. They may, for example, include making his bed, putting his clothes in the hamper, or taking out the trash. A weekly chart is kept and the parent and the child predecide how many tokens, for example, poker chips, the child will receive for performing as agreed. Whenever the child does do the work, he promptly receives the predecided number of poker chips. The child is allowed to accumulate the credits he earns for desirable behavior and can exchange them later for objects or for privileges he regards as desirable. In other

---

*Parents should *never* leave the house while the child is locked in the room, because of the always present (even though remote) possibility of fire or similar emergency.

words, he earns tokens and spends them for going to the movies, going out to play, watching TV, or, if the parents choose, even for money. In any event, the rate of exchange should also be decided upon beforehand. This technique will be further described in the subsection entitled "Chores."

These techniques may seem very mechanical to the parent who has diligently read books on child guidance and child rearing. Most of these books stress the fact that children misbehave because of deep-seated underlying problems, or lack of understanding of their own feelings. A valuable principle that has been taught us by the operant therapists is that although these statements can be true, children are also mightily influenced by the consequences of their acts. Love is not enough. Understanding is not enough. If a child is to learn to behave desirably, his parents must become aware of what their own reactions are in response to his various kinds of acts.

A child may behave well without understanding or he may misbehave with full insight into what he is doing. The child may accurately describe himself as angry when he hits his baby sister. This is an interesting instance of the child's ability to comment on his own behavior. It is not helpful to his baby sister. For the child to be helped, and for the family to be helped, the child must learn to control his own behavior. If the child is to feel good about himself he *may* also have to learn about his own feelings. Helping the child understand himself and deal with his feelings will be discussed in the next section.

HELPFUL GENERAL PRINCIPLES AND TECHNIQUES

The general question of how parents should treat their children, of how they should relate to them in order to produce the healthiest possible psychological environment, has been the subject of numerous books. Such books, of course, carry a wealth of helpful advice for parents of all kinds of children, and no effort can be made here to review all the approaches that psychologists have found useful. However, certain general principles and techniques that are of special benefit to HA children as well as to children with no problems will be discussed briefly. When added to the previous discussion of basic procedures, they provide a good picture of psychological approaches that can be particularly useful in the management of the HA child.*

1. How to Criticize

No one likes criticism. Children are no exception. Everyone can tolerate criticism best when it is specific, not generalized. For example, the husband who arrives home from work and finds supper not ready could respond with either of these two statements: "You are a terrible wife and never get anything done," or, "I'm always starving when I arrive home and I'd really appreciate it if you could have dinner ready when I got home." The wife might not like either of the two statements but the second, being more specific and somewhat more understanding, is a lot easier to take. Similarly, an employer faced with a problem of chastising an employee who is late finishing a piece of work could select one of the following statements: "Jones, you are a lousy worker," or, "Jones, I'd appreciate it in the future if you'd be faster in getting me these reports." Again, the employee may not like *any* criticism, but the second version, being specific, is easier to swallow.

The same principle applies to criticism of children. When, for example, the HA child has just hit his baby sister for picking up his favorite toy, reducing her to a howling mass, the parent is likely to explode and say such things as: "Why must you be such a bad child?" "You're a terrible child and you're always making trouble!" "Can't you do anything right?" That parents do this is understandable. Nevertheless, such an explosion is not helpful. If parents have thought about the problem areas in which improvement is wanted, they are in a far better position to criticize specifically. For example: "I told you not to hit your baby sister. That hurts her and makes me angry. Please go to your room." Other examples: "I do not like it when you eat with your hands— that is for small babies, not big children"; "Mommy gets upset when she asks you to clean up your room and you do not. No-

---

*For more discussion of these matters the parent might find it helpful to consult Haim G. Ginott's *Between Parent and Child* (New York: Avon, 1973).

body likes to look at messy rooms. Please go back and clean it." In the examples given, the parent expresses anger—but about *specific acts*. As will be discussed later, it is perfectly all right and it is sensible for the parent to acknowledge feelings that a child knows are present. The child can see that the parent is angry. Denying what the child knows is not useful. But let us repeat, the parents must not allow their anger to take the form of criticizing the child as a whole. The parents must never call the child worthless or bad. When criticism is necessary, the parents should criticize the objectionable behavior and be as specific as possible.

2. How to Praise

Similarly, praise should be specific. As discussed earlier, affectionate attention should be provided when the child is behaving desirably. If the child is eating nicely, say, "You are eating in a very grown-up fashion and that pleases me." If his baby sister is teasing him and he has resisted the urge to slug her, say, "I am very pleased that you can hold your temper even when Susie is making a pest of herself."

It is not very helpful to say, "You are a wonderful child," or to tell your spouse, "Jimmy has been just marvelous today." In addition to being ineffective in helping the child achieve self-control, such comments are likely to strike him as phony. All of us react to such comprehensive praise as false. We all know that we have our good points and our bad points and that anybody who calls us "wonderful" is either trying to butter us up or is stupid. Children have the same reaction. Consider the TV talk show in which an actor is introduced as a "wonderful personality." That turns most of us off. We recognize it for the hokum it is. Thus, when you do praise children, praise them for specific things that they have done that they know are good. Do not enlarge. Children recognize and appreciate honesty.

3. Recognizing the Child's Feelings

Haim Ginott's book *Between Parent and Child* is very well worth reading on this point. The general principle is that children, like adults, need to be understood, especially by someone important to them. Children have feelings. Recognizing those feelings and letting the child know that you recognize them often helps the child to feel better. It is extremely important, however, to realize that you can recognize a child's feelings and communicate your recognition of those feelings to the child without either criticizing or praising him. If he is returning from his room, where he has been sent because of lack of control, the parent can help the child by saying something like "You must have felt that it is very difficult for a seven-year-old to always remember his table manners, and you must have been angry at Mommy for making you leave the table."

By recognizing and acknowledging feelings in a neutral way, the parent can make the child feel more comfortable.

4. Helping the Child Distinguish Between Feelings and Actions
The major principle here is that feelings can and should be expressed, even if they are "bad." A part of the same principle is that feelings and actions are not the same thing. As we have mentioned earlier, children, like adults, often have feelings that "they should not"; they are sometimes envious, jealous, angry, resentful. All children have these feelings. In certain circumstances everyone has them. Children often feel guilty about having such feelings. They have learned that one "should not" be envious, jealous, angry, or resentful. It is very helpful if the parents, as discussed in the previous section, acknowledge to themselves that the child has such feelings (when he does) and let the child know that they (the parents) know. The parents must help the child distinguish between feelings (which are acceptable) and actions (which are not). Actions—that is, behavior—can be changed and shaped; feelings cannot be changed so directly and should not be treated as if they could be. If the child sees that his parents recognize and tolerate his feelings, his anxiety about having them may be relieved. His relief alone may often release enough "steam" so that the child will not act on his bad feelings. The child will feel less guilty if he knows that bad *thoughts* do not mean that he is bad and worthless in his parents' eyes. Since in the past he has *acted* in ways that have been considered unac-

ceptable, he is likely to regard having comparable thoughts as equally reprehensible. The parents should repeatedly communicate to the child, directly and indirectly, that any "bad thoughts" that he might have are not terrible so long as he does not act upon them. He will sometimes feel very angry at his baby sister; he should express such anger and his parents should help him express such angry *feelings*. He should not slug his baby sister. Parents should help the child to understand the difference between *thinking* and *doing*.

5. The Technique of Labeling

One extremely important technique in helping the HA child to recognize and do something about his behavioral problems is "labeling." Before the child can even begin to attempt to control his own behavior, he must know when he is doing something that is troublesome to others or hurtful to himself. The catch is that many of these things are rather complicated. It is easy for the parent to tell the child, "When you lie down on the floor, scream, and pound your heels, that is a tantrum," and "Mommy will not talk to you until the tantrum is over, and if you cannot make it stop quickly you will have to go to your room until it is over." A three-year-old can learn what a tantrum is. But some of the HA child's trouble-producing behaviors are more complex than that. For example, he may devise sophisticated techniques—and have a variety of them—for "bugging" his brother or sister. His father and mother cannot draw up a complete list of "bugging" behaviors. An enterprising, intelligent HA child can find multiple ways of annoying others. In order to help the child identify and recognize such behaviors, the parents should choose a "code word." The code words we use are "bugging" and "teasing." Every time the HA child bothers his brother or sister this way, the child is told, "You are teasing." After a few dozen repetitions—and parents will have many, many opportunities in the course of time—the child learns to recognize that a whole group of different things can be called "teasing." It is no harder for the child to learn this than it is for him to learn that Great Danes, Dachshunds, and Chihuahuas are all dogs.

Once the child has learned what teasing is, the parents can expand the usefulness of the procedure by dealing with new occurrences in a different way. When HA Billy is pretending that he has lost his sister's doll, the parent can say, "Billy, what are you doing?" The intention now is to have him label his own behavior, which is a step toward taking more responsibility for it.

Other examples of common problems for which labeling is a useful technique are "having trouble with attention" or "getting excited." Parents should actively look for and invent labels for the particular problems of their HA child that may lend themselves to this procedure. With repetitive labeling of this sort, the parents of the HA child can generally help him to identify what he is doing. It should be remembered that this is not easy. In *Games People Play,* Eric Berne spends a lot to time making up clever names for neurotic behaviors of adults. The reason the clever names are useful is that even adults, without the handicaps of HA, do not easily recognize the different ways in which they can be neurotic or just plain difficult. It is not surprising, then, that an immature ten-year-old will have a hard time learning what is objectionable about his behavior.

Scientific investigation of the usefulness of teaching children to recognize their own troublesome behavior is in an early stage. Interestingly, Russian child psychologists have for some time been examining the ways in which language can help a child to control himself. They feel that self-labeling is the first step in self-control, and that the sooner the child learns to label what he is doing, the sooner he can learn to control himself. Research in this area has only recently started in the United States, and definitive evidence is not yet available; however, our clinical experience has impressed us with the usefulness of labeling as an additional parental technique.

THE MANAGEMENT OF COMMON PROBLEMS
OF THE HA CHILD

The procedures, principles, and techniques described above refer to overall approaches to the HA child. In addition, we have some special suggestions that may be of help in managing a few specific common problems of the HA child.

1. Getting the Child's Attention

As we have mentioned, one of the HA child's major problems is paying attention. One of the major problems of the parent of an HA child is getting the child's attention. If one wishes to communicate effectively with an HA child, one must use some special techniques. For example, often the parent will give a command to or make a request of an HA preschooler while the child's attention is elsewhere. In non-HA children such a parental request may catch the child's attention. In the case of the HA child, it usually does not. Even if the parent *has* the HA child's attention, the child may not wish to hear what the parent has to say and may place his hands over his ears or turn his head away. The procedure that should be employed is as follows: the parent should take the HA child's head (or shoulders) gently in his (or her) hands and give the HA child the message. Then, to be sure that the child has received the message, the parent should ask the child what he was told, not in a punitive way but with a neutral tone. If the child does not know, the parent should make the statement again. Physical contact seems to play an important role in gaining the child's attention. We do not know why, but when the message is given with the parent's hands placed on the child's shoulders, the child seems to pay better attention than he does when not touched.

Although the instructions above have mentioned the preschooler, physical contact may still be useful with the older child as well. The procedure of asking the child what it is that he was told is also useful for the older child. Parents should remember that if they find themselves yelling in order to get the child's attention, something has gone wrong someplace.

2. Rigidity

A characteristic of some HA children—although it can be seen in non-HA children as well—is "rigidity." Rigid children are upset when their activities are interrupted or their routines are changed. For example, they may become furious if they are stopped from playing with their toys in order to be taken on a visit to Grandma's. Or they may begin screaming if the order of putting on their clothes is varied. One three-year-old HA child had a tantrum if the family drove to Grandma's house by a different route.

Rigidity sometimes disappears with age, but there are effective ways of dealing with it before that blessed time comes. The major principle is anticipation. Long before the break in routine occurs, the parent should repeatedly tell the child what is going to happen. For example, if he is playing with his blocks and cars and the time to leave for Grandma's is two hours in the future, the parent should begin a countdown, as in a NASA moonshot: "Billy, we will be visiting Grandma in two hours." Then, an hour later, "We will be leaving in one hour. It's time for you to put the trucks away." Next, "Billy, we are leaving for Grandma's in 15 minutes. It's time to put the blocks away, change your clothes, and put your shoes on." With older children, to avoid repeated nagging, egg timers can be invaluable. Even before the child can tell time, he can recognize when the pointer is approaching the "0" that will start the bell. Rather than giving countdowns every morning for getting dressed to go to school, one can substitute the timer.

Similarly, considerable grief can often be avoided by discussing long-term changes before they occur. Repeated anticipatory discussions of such matters as furniture moving, new sleeping arrangements, and altered school programs can frequently soften the blow for the rigid child. These procedures, of course, do not change the child's rigidity, but they lessen the unpleasant impact of that rigidity.

3. Spiraling Loss of Control

A very frequent problem of HA children, both as preschoolers and during the first few grades, is a "spiraling" loss of behavioral control. This refers to the child's becoming increasingly wild and behaving more and more immaturely once he is "set off." For example, when guests come, the child may act in an attention-seeking manner, and as soon as he gets the attention he may react with foolish and noisy behavior that steadily worsens. After first telling the guests a story or showing them some of his models, he may begin to talk more loudly, to start running around, and in some instances to bounce off the walls. This may also happen in noisy or stimulating situations, such as the supermarket or the circus.

How can this loss of control be handled? To begin with, parents will spare themselves considerable grief if they learn to recognize the early symptoms of this behavioral breakdown. It is far easier to reverse such cycles shortly after they have started than when they are in full swing. When the parents recognize the symptoms of an impending behavior spiral, they should caution the child with a phrase that is always used when the child is excited—and here we see again the labeling technique in operation. Different parents use different phrases. Some parents will say, "You are getting too wild," while others might say, "You are becoming overexcited." The important point is to label the same kind of behavior in the same way every time so that the child can learn what the parents mean by the special phrase. After the parent has identified the behavior, the child should be told to go to his own room and to remain there until he has calmed down. If necessary, he should be taken to his room. Once he has calmed down, the child should receive no punishment but should in fact receive praise for having gotten control of himself, and for now acting like a big boy. Then, in a nonaccusatory tone of voice, the parent should explain to the child what happened before and what caused the parent to label that behavior as "wild" or "overexcited." In other words, parents should make sure that the child is praised (gets positive reinforcement) for acting quite grown-up, and that the child receives no extra attention—positive or negative—for being out of control.

Thus, the best thing to do about spiraling loss of control is to try to avoid it. To use a variation on an old cliché, parents should be ready with that invaluable ounce of prevention. They should learn to recognize the situations that trigger these spiraling reactions and either avoid them or remove the child from them as soon as possible.

4. Verbal Tantrums
One of the kinds of loss of control seen in both younger and

older HA children is the "verbal tantrum." Such behavior is probably more "mature" than breath-holding spells or down-on-the-floor-kicking tantrums, but parents are not overjoyed at this kind of maturation. During the tantrum the child may talk (or yell) continuously, criticizing, blaming others, and denying responsibility. He may bring up not only trivial matters but honest-to-goodness problems that exist in the family. The nonstop productions are limited only by his talkativeness and how his parents handle the problem. The natural reaction of most parents is to argue. The major advice that we have is that the parent should not argue at all. A mutual screaming match solves nothing. While the child is having the tantrum, he should be told that matters will be discussed when he quiets down. If he is unable to quiet down, he should be placed in a "time out" room, and only *after* he quiets down should the parent talk with the child about the real problem. As we pointed out with regard to the problem of getting the child's attention, parents who frequently find themselves yelling can interpret that as a warning sign that they are doing something wrong—not bad, just ineffective.

5. Chores

Although particular chores have been used as examples in the preceding sections, we are giving special attention to the entire subject of getting the child to do routine, age-appropriate chores because it is one of the most common causes of friction between the school-age HA child and his parents. At first, nonperformance may be a result of forgetfulness and the child's inability to organize well. If the parents become angry and nag—and except for a few saints, most become angry—the child may become increasingly stubborn and negative. This may lead to a snowballing of complaints by the parents and of gold-bricking by the child.

The best way to make sure that chores are done is as follows. First, list all the chores that you want the child to do. Second, arrange them in order of importance ("1" next to the most important task, "2" next to the second most important task, and so forth). Then, *write down* one or two of the most important chores on a homemade calendar and place this calendar in a conspicuous place, say, on the door of the refrigerator. For example, if one chore is to set the table every other day (as sometimes happens when a brother or sister is also doing the same chore), the calendar should have the child's name listed on each day he is to perform it. If there are two chores involved, such as setting the table and clearing the table, each should be listed separately on the day it is to be done (whether every day, on alternate days, or according to some other schedule).

As indicated earlier, parents should avoid any disputes about what constitutes the chore by writing down specific components of the chore. In setting the table, does one only have to place the silverware and dishes, or does one also have to bring the butter and milk from the refrigerator, and so forth? Assuming reasonably good parent-child relationships, many children will be compliant about chores if the requests are specific and structured enough.

If the child is resistant, the behavior modification principles we have mentioned should be employed. For example, parents could establish a rule saying that full payment of allowance will be made only if setting the table is done, without nagging, six times a week. With such a rule, if the chore is done only five times in a week, the child is "docked" in some mutually agreed-upon way—such as receiving only five-sixths of his allowance.

After the most important chores are being done on a regular basis, the parents can move on to the next chore. Again, the calendar should be kept, and directions should be very clear and specific. Parents will avoid "hassles" if the rules are easy to understand and clear-cut. If they are not, the opportunity for legal arguments is much greater. And as all parents know, most children are born lawyers.

6. Having the Child Take Responsibility for Himself

All parents hope that eventually the child will take responsibility for monitoring his own behavior. The procedure discussed under "Chores" illustrates one way of establishing a habit of responsibility. Here we will provide an illustration of another method of encouraging responsibility. The example deals with another recurrent problem of the HA child—forgetting to bring his school assignments home, which means that he does not do his homework.

For this problem, we suggest that the child be given a small notebook in which he must write down *every day* after arriving home from school the work he actually accomplished at school and what was left undone in each subject that day. If homework assignments are given, he should write down those assignments while he is in school, in the same book. It is his responsibility to write this information down. At the end of the week, the parent should contact the child's teacher to make sure that the child did accurately record the completed work, the daily work that he did not finish in school, and the assigned homework. The trick with this technique is making the child responsible for "telling on himself." We find that if the child reports accurately, he will be in a better position to proceed with the unfinished work and the homework, and he is more likely to complete both kinds of assignments after school. If the child fails to write the information down, he is "docked" part of his allowance or other privileges. In some instances, it may be better to start with a smaller allowance and to "reinforce" the child by giving him an agreed-upon bonus when he writes down the assignments correctly. After the child has mastered these tasks completely, the parents can often gradually withdraw the "reinforcement" and return to the usual allowance. After the notebook procedure has continued several weeks, the parents need only "spot check" with the teacher. However, as is the case for most responsibilities expected of most HA children, the child should continue to use self-monitoring techniques long after his behavior is satisfactory. It is our impression that by really overdoing these techniques, parents can finally depend on the child to maintain some behavior patterns without such external supports.

Although the example has concerned school assignments, analogous procedures—with notebooks or calendars—can be worked out for such areas of the child's life as personal hygiene, grooming, music and dancing lessons, and so forth.

SPECIAL PSYCHOLOGICAL HELP
FOR THE FAMILY AND CHILD

From time to time we have referred to the fact that in some families—either because of the presence of the HA child or for entirely different reasons—there will be much family stress and strain. As we have mentioned, such family difficulties cause problems for any child and they may cause greater problems for the HA child. If the parents cannot agree between themselves as to rules for their children, if they do not consistently reward and punish, if they criticize one child or favor another because of their own personal problems, they will create psychological difficulties for their children. Obviously, families with disturbances need professional help, regardless of whether they have a hyperactive child, and this is the kind of situation in which help can be provided by psychiatrists, social workers, or psychologists. Any steps that will decrease difficulties within the family will be of special benefit to the hyperactive child, since adjustment to even ordinary social demands is already difficult for him. Even if he responds well to medication, he may not respond to emotional stress as flexibly as a child who is not hyperactive.

As we briefly mentioned earlier, another form of specific psychological help that is *sometimes* useful for the HA child is psychotherapy, in which the child meets with a therapist, either individually or with other children in a group. The purposes of psychotherapy are to enable a child to recognize and understand his feelings and to learn to deal with them appropriately. Psychotherapy is a very popular and indeed fashionable mode of treatment. In the past it has been considered to be the best treatment for virtually all psychiatric difficulties both in adults and in children. Currently, however, one of the major questions in adult and child psychiatry concerns the effectiveness of psychotherapy for particular kinds of problems. There are no data whatsoever supporting the usefulness of psychotherapy in the basic treatment of hyperactive children. Nonetheless, many experienced psychiatrists have found that it is sometimes a useful auxiliary technique with *some* HA children. In our own experience it has been most useful in older HA children and especially in those older children who have "engrafted" psychological disabilities upon their "temperamental" ones. Many of the difficulties of these children are in the area of interpersonal relations, and we have received the *impression* that psychotherapy has proved useful with some of these children some of the time. These have generally been HA children who did not receive treatment with medication in their earlier years and as a result fell into the vicious circle of school and familial problems. They seem to have benefited from a relationship with a warm and impartial adult who was able to provide them with some understanding of their problems and help them in the construction of solutions to these problems.

Certainly individual psychotherapy is *not* the treatment of choice for most HA children. Unfortunately, the usefulness of medication and the other techniques discussed has only recently been realized. In the past many HA children received psychotherapy, and for most of them it apparently was not helpful. Since it is a time-consuming and expensive procedure, it should only be used when there is a strong possibility that working with the child's special problems may be useful, or when the child seems unresponsive to all other forms of treatment. This is certainly an area of hot dispute and many psychiatrists would undoubtedly disagree with us. All we can state is that we have seen dozens of hyperactive children who have received psychotherapy, often for years, with no visible benefit, and who subsequently responded dramatically to treatment with medication. As has been repeatedly stated, the basis of most HA children's problems is physiological and must be dealt with physiologically, that is, with the aid of medication. Medication gets to the root of the problem. Psychotherapy may help to deal with some of the branches which, so to speak, have grown in the wrong direction. Many parents do not feel this way. We remember one very sophisticated mother whose seriously afflicted HA child had responded dramatically to medication. At the first visit after medicine had been started the mother reported, "Tim is 100 percent better, Doctor. Now let's put him in psychotherapy and really get to the root of the problem."

Although psychotherapy is occasionally useful in some HA children, simpler measures should be employed first. If medication, educational remediation, and parental counseling fail to help the child as much as seems necessary, psychotherapy can be tried.

VACATIONS FOR THE PARENTS

Living with difficult children is difficult. The techniques we have discussed may make parents' lives easier, but their lives may still be much harder than the lives of most parents. For this reason we think that it is very important for the parents of HA children to get away sometimes by themselves. (It is probably highly desirable for *all* parents. It is essential for the parents of HA children.) It is not a sign of intellectual, moral, or physical weakness for these parents to want a periodic vacation by themselves. HA children demand much attention, and caring for them can be physically, mentally, and emotionally exhausting. In addition, sometimes the parents' relationship suffers as a result of the tension surrounding the child's problems. The happiness and well-being of everyone should not be sacrificed for the good of the child with problems. Everyone deserves a piece of the pie. Thus, it is an excellent practice for parents to schedule regular time-out periods for themselves.

Obviously, such vacations pose practical problems. The HA child is often too much of a handful to deposit with unsuspecting relatives. If the community has an organization for parents of HA children, it might offer opportunities to share child care, with the parents taking turns at vacations without the children. Such trading has the advantage that all the adults involved are aware of the problems of the HA child and have some knowledge of how to handle those problems. This kind of trading off is not just of selfish value to the parents. If they are able to spend some time alone with each other and to enjoy themselves, they may be more relaxed in handling their HA child when they return, and this would benefit the child (and other children in the family as well). But whether or not this is the case, it is sufficient that the parents themselves will feel better.

Educational Management

As has been previously discussed, HA children frequently experience academic difficulties, difficulties that seem to arise from two major sources. First, most HA children are apt to have some problems in learning because of their distractibility, lack of stick-to-itiveness, readiness to give up, tendency to rush through things, and inability to discipline themselves. (The last is particularly important—at least to parents; an almost constant complaint among the parents of older HA children is their failure to do their homework. For special help here, see the earlier section, "Having the Child Take Responsibility for Himself.") *Some* HA children also have the specific perceptual difficulties (reversals, etc.) that are called learning disabilities.

There are therefore two groups of HA children with learning problems: (1) those whose learning problems are secondary only to distractibility and inattentiveness; and (2) those whose learning difficulties are secondary to these inattention difficulties and also to specific perceptual problems. Medication sometimes eliminates and frequently diminishes learning problems, particularly in the first group of children. However, even among those in whom the learning problems diminish with medication, additional educational assistance is often needed. Too often, by the time the child's academic problems are recognized and treated, the HA child has fallen behind in many subjects. Learning problems are cumulative. Consequently, the child cannot compensate for his educational losses, despite improved functioning, unless remedial tutoring is provided in those areas in which he has fallen behind. The problem of cumulative educational lacks is most severe in those HA children whose difficulties are first recognized in adolescence. They have often received "social promotions" and are apt to be several grade levels behind in a number of subjects. Unfortunately, although medication may still be effective, appropriate educational facilities are often not available, and these children, frustrated and embarrassed by their poor academic showing, tend to give up. We will have a few suggestions for this group of children toward the end of this chapter.

The children with specific perceptual deficits are another problem. It seems to be the case that medicine *may* improve their attention span and stick-to-itiveness, but does not remedy their perceptual difficulties. The special educational problems of children with these perceptual difficulties—that is, with learning disabilities—will be discussed in chapter 6.

Since many educators do not recognize HA children as a unique category, they frequently place such children in special educational classes, even though the children have no specific perceptual problems. In addition, many of the children placed in these classes have both hyperactivity problems *and* perceptual difficulties. In both types of children a trial of medication is generally useful. To repeat, there is no way of predicting a child's response, and one may anticipate that some of the problems will disappear whereas others (including the perceptual ones) may remain. A further point that might be made here is that any child who has been placed in a special class without a specific diagnosis of his difficulties is possibly hyperactive; such a child should be carefully evaluated to see if he is hyperactive and therefore eligible for a trial of medication.

It is probably useful to mention some "educational" approaches that have been employed but have not demonstrated effectiveness. A number of people had noticed that there were some children who had both learning problems and coordination problems. (As was mentioned earlier, approximately half of HA children do have some coordination problems.) These people reasoned, erroneously, that the learning problems were probably the result of the coordination problems. (Both are probably the result of a third factor.) They reasoned also that if the learning problems were the result of coordination problems, training in coordination might improve the learning difficulties. For this reason they prescribed exercises, involving either the whole body or the eyes. *At the present time there is no evidence whatsoever that coordination training will help the HA child's learning difficulties.* The same statement applies to specific treatment programs of eye exercises.

However, coordination training *may* help the HA child's coordination problems. The coordination difficulties from which many HA children suffer are frequently embarrassing or humiliating to the child. This is particularly true for boys. To be chosen last when teams are being picked, and to be ridiculed for his athletic inadequacy, is a blow to the HA boy's already shaky self-esteem. There are programs in physical reeducation—not readily available—in which the children receive specific tutoring in motor tasks of increasing difficulty. It is our impression that these programs sometimes improve the child's coordination and generally increase his self-confidence. If such programs are not available, the parent may help the poorly coordinated HA child by guiding him toward physical activity in which fine coordination presents less of a problem. As mentioned, many HA children have particular problems with hand-eye coordination and as a result are worst in sports such as baseball and tennis. Sometimes they encounter less difficulty in football—particularly in line play, where gross body movement is required—or in basketball. These children may often perform adequately or excellently in sports requiring large muscle control, such as running and swimming. Judo also seems a good sport for the hyperactive child; even though he may not do as well as the nonhyperactive child, he can acquire skills that give him the novel feeling of being a "big man," a feeling that often considerably bolsters his self-esteem.

Special Problems of Adolescence

The HA child whose problem is first discovered in adolescence poses several practical problems. The first is that the child has already had years of unhappy experience as a result of his hyperactivity. The second major problem is that adolescence is a time of rebellion for most children, hyperactive or otherwise. Since the child is now increasingly independent, his cooperation in the treatment program is absolutely necessary. Furthermore, the behavioral techniques we have discussed are more useful with pre-adolescent children.

On the positive side of the ledger, the adolescent is in a better position to understand and recognize the basis of his difficulties. This understanding, if it can be obtained, may balance out the other problems. From a practical standpoint, helping the adolescent HA child generally requires that more time be spent by the treating physician in seeing the adolescent individually, or with his family as part of family therapy.

If the HA adolescent has had serious learning problems, the situation may be critical. If he is five years behind in reading and spelling, school will be a nightmare to him. It is often difficult and sometimes impossible to convince such an adolescent that he is not a "retard." If he can be convinced that he has reading problems that are not associated with intelligence (a condition sometimes called "dyslexia"), that he is not a moron, half the battle has been won. The second half is more difficult to accomplish. He must be entered in some kind of program in which his abilities will allow him to succeed and in which his disabilities will not seriously penalize him. If the public schools available to the youngster do not have the flexibility to help him explore the areas in which he might do well, it might be desirable for the parents to look for a private school that offers more options.

There is an educational technique that makes use of audio tapes, which will be discussed in chapter 6 (on learning disabilities), which could conceivably be of particular usefulness with this group of youngsters. If researchers and parents do find that youngsters with reading problems can learn subject content more easily by listening to such tapes, the next step would be to convince educational systems to use such procedures on a larger scale.

Summary

In capsule form we would like to repeat the major points of this chapter.

First, most HA children respond to medication. *All* HA children deserve a trial of medication since there is absolutely no way of predicting which children will respond well and which children will not respond well. *Sometimes* medication alone is enough. Since the prescription of medication requires a doctor, a physician must always be involved in the treatment of the HA child.

Second, changes in the relationship between the parents and the HA child are almost always helpful. Understanding and the establishment of firm, consistent, explicit, predictable rules are always useful. Frequently these can be achieved with little or no professional help. On some occasions the assistance of a third party (psychiatrist, psychologist, or social worker) may be helpful.

Third, *some* HA children need special educational assistance.

In many instances this will only be remedial education, while in some instances it may be "special education" (see chapter 6).

With such interventions, most HA children can be helped, often to a substantial degree. Not only will these forms of intervention help to diminish the present problems of HA children, but also they will often help to prevent future ones.

6

Learning Disabilities: Description and Recommendations

Learning disabled is the term applied to children who have problems with reading, spelling, or arithmetic despite the fact that they have approximately normal intelligence and have no psychiatric or environmental problems that account for the learning difficulties. For reasons that are as yet unexplained, the learning disabled child's brain seems to perceive, process, or remember certain kinds of mental tasks in a faulty manner.

If a child has a problem in thinking or perceiving that does not affect his or her schoolwork, that problem is not called a learning disability even though the basic underlying difficulty may be similar. For example, tone deafness may be a problem similar to learning disability. Tone deaf children—and adults—perceive and perform music differently from the average person. Tone deaf people, unlike most other people, are unable to reproduce with reasonable accuracy a pitch that they hear. The tone deaf person has intact hearing yet is unable to tell whether or not the sound of his (or her) voice is exactly the same as the pitch that he hears. The tone deaf person has great difficulty singing in tune and has trouble playing an instrument in which the pitch has to be regulated on the basis of what is heard—for example, a violin or trombone. Tone deafness is not referred to as a learning disability because being able to sing in tune or play an instrument in tune is not part of the required school curriculum. If it were part of the school curriculum then tone deaf people would probably be considered learning disabled.

This analogy to tone deafness may help people understand what is meant by learning disability. Tone deaf people are not brain-damaged and there is nothing wrong with their hearing. Nobody would suggest that tone deafness is due to laziness, poor teaching, or poor motivation. It is true that if a person has no interest in music he will not put forth the effort to train himself in the direction of better pitch perception. In this sense, motivation is related to one's ability to overcome the problem. But the basic difficulty is somehow related to brain function, even though there is no severe disturbance such as brain damage.

Much of what we have said about tone deafness is also true of learning disability. The field of learning disability is much more complex, however, because of the great variety of problems in perception or thinking that affect reading, writing, spelling, and mathematics. For the most part, specialists in child development have a very poor understanding of just what those problems are (though they are gradually learning more about them).

Because it is not clear exactly what the underlying problem is, learning disability is recognized by the fact that the child performs much more poorly in one of the academic subjects than would be expected on the basis of his learning ability or I.Q. One should suspect a learning disability, therefore, whenever a child seems unable to read, spell, or compute anywhere near as well as would be expected on the basis of his other abilities. When a specialist examines a child suspected of having learning disability, the testing involves measuring the basic learning ability—that is, the I.Q.—and then testing the child's achievement levels in reading, spelling, arithmetic, and handwriting to see how they compare to the basic learning ability. An average child who is performing at a level substantially below average may have a learning disability, but so may a bright child who is performing at an average level. People are less likely to be concerned about a child with average performance, but if it is much lower than would be expected on the basis of his or her intelligence, the child might well have a learning disability. Learning disabilities appear in children of different intelligence levels, ranging all the way from the brilliant to the mildly retarded. (In the person with more severe retardation, it may be impossible to separate the learning disability from signs of below normal intelligence.)

The question of when underachievement should be interpreted as learning disability is something that the experts debate. Usually such a judgment is made somewhat arbitrarily when the child's performance is approximately two years behind that expected for his level of intelligence. For example, a ten-year-old fourth-grader with an average I.Q. of 100 would be expected to read and do arithmetic at the 4.0 grade level. If he could read and do arithmetic at only the 2.0 grade level, he would be said to have learning disability. If he could read at only the 2.0 grade level but could do arithmetic at the 3.0 level, it might be assumed that his learning disability was largely in the area of reading and that his reading disability was perhaps affecting his arithmetic performance. To take another example, if a ten-year-old fourth-grader had an I.Q. of 90, then standardization tables might indicate that he should be reading and doing arithmetic at the 3.5 grade level. If he could read and do arithmetic at the 2.0 grade level he would *not* be considered as learning disabled. These kinds of standards can be applied to children in the third grade or higher (who might be functioning, say, at a first-grade level). Obviously, they cannot be applied to younger children, who have not had two years' exposure to school, because achievement tests are based upon exposure to a standard school curriculum.

The reader may be asking at this point, "Don't other problems besides learning disability cause children to underachieve in school subjects?" Though the answer is obviously "Yes," many specialists think that underachieving by as much as two years is seldom produced by anything other than a learning disability unless the child is quite severely disturbed (as in autistic or schizophrenic children) or has been severely deprived environmentally.

Though underachievement is the most reliable indicator of possible learning disability, there are other kinds of suggestive evidence. Learning disabled children *may* also perform their reading, spelling, or arithmetic in a qualitatively different way, producing characteristic kinds of errors. The presence of these typical errors may suggest learning disability. There is as yet no way to evaluate these typical errors reliably, so the conclusions reached are still subjective, depending on the personal interpretation of the tester.

We will indicate below some of the different kinds of errors that are seen among learning disabled children, producing difficulties in reading, spelling, handwriting, and arithmetic. It is important to remember that there is great variety in learning disabilities, and that a particular child may have some of the disabilities we will describe but none of the others. Thus, we will repeatedly emphasize that areas in which some learning disabled children have difficulty are no problem for children with other kinds of learning disabilities. The outstanding point to be made in this entire discussion is the importance of evaluating the child in terms of his own strengths and weaknesses. The pattern may be different for each child.

Some children have more difficulty than others in seeing the difference between letters or short words that are alike except for their differing orientation in space. In order to be able to recognize the letter "b," one must always see that letter with the "stick part" facing up and the "round part" facing right. As we mentioned earlier, young children have difficulty distinguishing left from right, and some HA children and learning disabled children seem to be slow in learning the difference. If one confuses right with left, or even up with down, a "b" may be confused with a "p" or a "d," or a "p" may be confused with a "q." If the child confuses the first and last letters, "was" becomes "saw." Learning disabled children sometimes seem to have a way of looking at letters and words without regarding their spatial orientation. This way of perceiving is a little easier to understand when one recalls that this is the way all of us look at *objects*. For example, a chair is a chair, whether it is upside down, pointing right or left, or on its side. But "b" and "was" are only "b" and "was" when they have one special orientation in space. If "b" is rotated, it can become a "p," a "q," or a "d," and "was" can become "saw."

Most very young, preschool children seem to look at letters

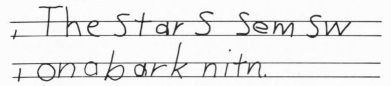

Fig. 1. A third-grader wrote this sentence to dictation. Translated it reads, "The stars seem small on a dark night." Note the inverted "m" in the word "small" ("sw") and the reversed "d" in the word "dark" ("bark").

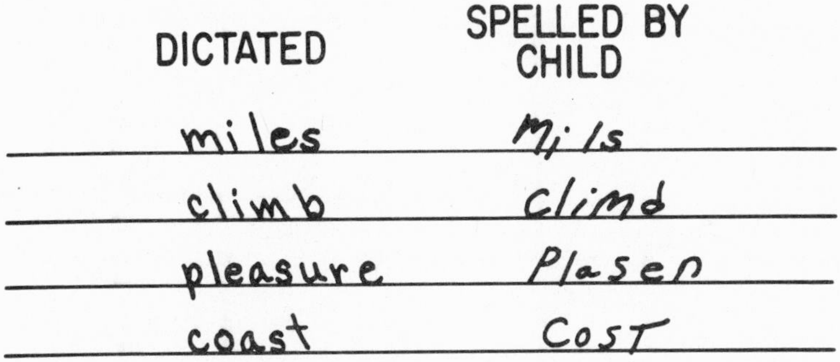

DICTATED	SPELLED BY CHILD
miles	Mils
climb	climd
pleasure	Plasen
coast	CosT

Fig. 2. Note how this ten-year-old child spells words as they sound, unable to "see" that the words do not look right.

and words as they would at objects (this may be the origin of the phrase "mind your p's and q's") and have difficulty distinguishing between letters whose identification depends on their spatial orientation. At around the age of six, the average child begins to perceive that the identity of certain letters and words depends on their orientation in space. This skill is absolutely essential for the recognition of some letters, and therefore it is a prerequisite for spelling and reading with facility. The learning disabled child apparently develops this skill much more slowly (see Fig. 1). This corresponds to our previous comment that in some ways HA children function as younger children do.

In addition, before one can learn to read or spell easily, one must be able to recognize words by sight and to remember how they look. That is, in order to read quickly one must be able to just glance at a word and recognize it without having to analyze it letter by letter. Conversely, in order to spell, one must have an image in one's mind of how the word looks when correctly writc̲at   s̲ee   r̲ed   t̲o   b̲ig   w̲ork

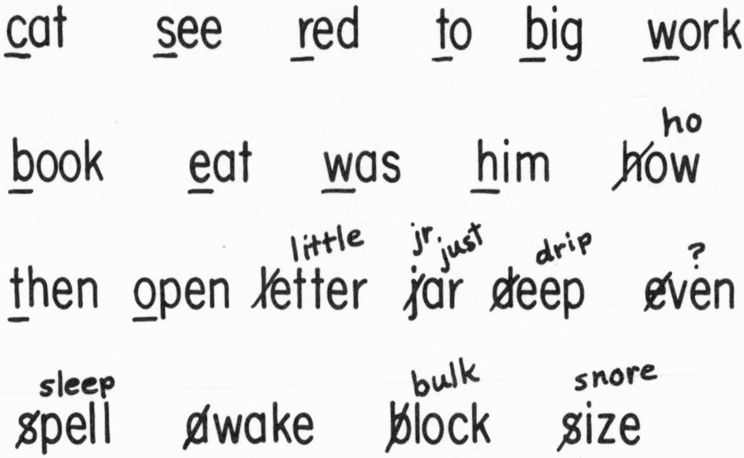

                              ho
b̲ook   e̲at   w̲as   h̲im   h̶ow

                 little jr just   drip   ?
t̲hen o̲pen l̶etter j̶ar d̶eep e̶ven

  sleep   bulk   snore
s̶pell   a̶wake   b̶lock   s̶ize

Fig. 3. This fourth-grader stops reading correctly as the words become more irregular in their spelling. For example, he does not recognize at a glance the common word "how" and sounds it out to "ho." Note also the reversed letter order involved in reading "spell" as "sleep."

ten or printed. This is especially true for people learning to read and write English because English is strikingly nonphonetic and the spelling often has little to do with the sound. Thus, in reading nonphonetic words, sounding out the letters would only slow down one's recognition of the word. Similarly, one cannot write nonphonetic words correctly from dictation, or in a composition or letter, without remembering how they look (see Fig. 2).

The normal child apparently has the ability to see whole words as pictures in his mind's eye. Learning disabled children are often deficient in this ability, that is, they must analyze words, letter by letter, because they do not immediately recognize them as whole units. They also have difficulty retaining a visual image of the sequence of letters in words. Figure 3 illustrates the problem, including an example of the word "spell" misread as "sleep." In part this problem seems associated with right-left, or reversal, difficulty. Interestingly, Japanese children who learn traditional Japanese, in which symbols stand for words, do not have this difficulty because there are no Japanese symbols that have a different meaning if seen backward.

A third problem of many learning disabled children has to do with hearing the sequence of sounds in words and then remembering these sounds in the correct order. For example, according to the phonetic method, in order to sound out the word "stop," one must retain in their correct sequence the "s" sound, then the "t" sound, next the "o" sound, and then the "p" sound, finally blending them appropriately into the entire word. Children with learning disability often have great difficulty with this kind of task. Even if they identify the individual sounds and letters correctly, by the time they get to the "o" and "p" sounds, they may have forgotten the order of the "s" and "t" sounds and end up spelling or reading a jumbled version of the word, such as t-o-s-p, "tosp." Possibly general problems of memory, which we will discuss later, are associated with this difficulty.

Children with this problem frequently also have difficulty hearing the sounds inside words. The more similar the sounds, the greater the difficulty, so that short vowel sounds are most frequently confused. For example, when asked to spell a word such as "dress," the child may have trouble hearing whether the vowel sound is an "e," an "a," or a "u." Obviously it is hard to learn to associate certain sounds with certain images if the sounds are confused. If the child hears "pat" both for the word "pet" and for the word "pat," he is going to become confused. This is often called an "auditory discrimination" problem; however, it is interesting that learning disabled children may demonstrate these difficulties only when listening to the sounds associated with letters and words and may have no trouble at all with other kinds of sounds. It does not seem to be a conventional problem in hearing. Children with this difficulty can hear faint sounds well, but they have trouble distinguishing between similar sounds whether they are soft or loud.

Children with these sounding-out problems make the following kinds of errors (in addition to using the wrong letters): (1) they drop out major sounds when spelling words (example: writing "odor" instead of "order"); (2) they add sounds that aren't there (example: "olpen" instead of "open"); (3) they turn the sounds

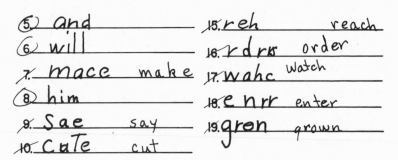

Fig. 4. This one sample of spelling from a third-grader illustrates many of the so-called auditory problems. In the word "reach" (15) the important "c" is dropped and also the silent "a." In the word "order" (16) both vowels are omitted. In the word "enter" (18) the major "t" sound is dropped.

around (example: "snip" instead of "spin"); (4) they drop out the understood vowels (example: "plantr" instead of "planter") (see Fig. 4).

These are some of the fundamental problems that accompany and *may* cause reading and spelling difficulties. Teachers and parents frequently categorize these problems as "visual" or "auditory" problems. Children with so-called "visual difficulties" are able to learn the phonetic method of reading once they have passed the hurdle of learning the letters. When they encounter a word they have not seen before, they are capable of sounding it out. But they are the ones who seem to lack a visual memory for the "pictures" of words and seem unable to remember the illogical way in which letters are put together to form some nonphonetic English words. Conversely, children with "auditory problems" seem incapable of learning the phonetic techniques of sounding out new words. When they encounter a word they have not seen before, they are at a loss as to how to sound it out properly. However, they sometimes have a good visual memory and can read what they have encountered frequently before, the words they have memorized, both the regular, phonetic words and the irregular, nonphonetic ones. Most children with learning disabilities have neither purely auditory nor purely visual problems. Most learning disabled children have both kinds of prob-

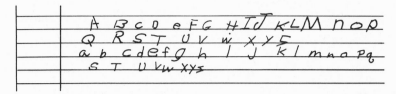

Fig. 5. This ten-year-old child was asked to write the alphabet. He has obvious difficulties with size and placement of letters. The writing process was also very slow—a typical problem.

lems, although they may have one to a larger degree than the other.

The child with learning disability often also has handwriting problems. Such children typically have difficulty translating what they see into the appropriate hand motions required to form the letters. Sometimes this difficulty is called a "visual-motor perceptual problem." In some instances, the problem seems to arise from difficulty with the fine motor coordination involved in using the small muscles of the hand to guide the pencil. However, the same child may have no difficulty playing the piano or using a typewriter, which illustrates again how very specific some of these problems seem to be.

Sometimes the handwriting problem seems more closely related to difficulties in perceiving the differences between letters. In other words, rather than involving a coordination problem, it involves difficulty in making the fine visual distinctions between similar letter forms. Whatever the basic underlying cause may be, what we usually *see* is slow, deliberate hand movements, with distortion in the placement, size, and shape of the letters (see Fig. 5).

In the area of arithmetic, the following problems are often seen: first, the same children who have difficulty with the spatial orientation of letters and words also have difficulty with the spatial orientation of math computation. For example, they have a hard time remembering whether problems are to be computed beginning at the right or the left, or remembering the top to bottom

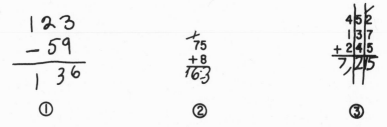

①   ②   ③

Fig. 6. These three problems illustrate some of the math difficulties experienced by learning disabled children. In the first problem the child subtracts the top number from the bottom one. In the second problem he adds across columns as well as along them. The 8 and the 5 are correctly added, and then he combines the 8 and the 7, adding the carried 1. The third problem is computed from left to right (rather than right to left). The child carried the 1 from the sum of the middle column (12) to the right column, summed that to 15, and concluded with 7,215.

relationship of subtraction. They may also have difficulty changing from working with columns in addition and subtraction to working with the different types of spatial orientation required in multiplication and division. They may have difficulty with the borrowing and carrying process, again because of right/left confusion. They may begin the computation from the left, or they may confuse number units, such as reading "41" as "14."

A different kind of problem develops in children who are very slow to learn the abstractions involved in arithmetic. Such children continue to have to use their fingers or other concrete helping aids much longer than the average child. One would think that this problem was closely related to intelligence, but a child who remains concrete in his mathematical thinking may possess excellent verbal intelligence, including the ability to think abstractly in the verbal sphere (see Fig. 6).

Frequently a very poor memory accompanies all these problems. For example, the child who has difficulty perceiving the spatial orientation of letters may work very hard to learn one particular letter only to forget it by the next hour or day. The same phenomenon may occur with each of the learning problems we have discussed—for example, remembering the images of nonphonetic words, or remembering the multiplication tables or the rules for long division. Memory in other areas, however, may be excellent. For example, many learning disabled children have a good artistic imagination, and many have an excellent mechanical sense. They may have an excellent memory for the way an object looks, or the way an engine is put together, at the same time that they have a seriously deficient memory when it comes to letters and words. This explains why parents and teachers are often puzzled by the discrepancy between the child's talents in some areas and striking deficiencies in others. The cause of poor memory in certain specific areas is not well understood. It *may* simply have to do with attentiveness. If a child does not pay attention to certain material, he does not learn it well. The memory problem may also result from a real deficiency and is possibly a manifestation of the chemical imbalance that may underlie some forms of hyperactivity.

As we began to describe these typical problems, we said that there were no good standardized tests that could be used to demonstrate these qualitative deficiencies. Achievement tests do show the *quantitative* problems, that is, the degree of disability, as indicated by how far a child is behind, but not the way the child performs each task. The best way to find the qualitative problems is to examine relevant schoolwork that the child is asked to do during the evaluation session. With any of the problems involving letters and words, a good way to assess typical errors is to inspect samples of the child's *unrehearsed* spelling. Often when we ask parents to bring us samples of the child's spelling, they bring the results of the child's weekly spelling test from school. This is not a good way to demonstrate the problem because in the typical spelling test the child has had considerable opportunity to study the words just prior to the test. It is important to know how he does with the same words a month later. The fairly bright learning disabled child may be able to get 100 percent on the weekly spelling test but may retain only a small percentage of those words a few weeks later.

Asking a child to read will usually also reveal specific problems; however, reading involves not only deciphering individual words but obtaining meaning from the sentence or the paragraph as a whole. The brighter child will begin to learn to assist himself in the reading process by using clues he gets from the meaning of the sentence. If, for example, he is reading the sentence, "The boy went for a walk by the lake," and he has trouble deciphering the word "walk," he is assisted considerably by contextual clues. The phrase "went for a ———" followed by "by the lake" limits one to a very few words that will make sense. In addition to "walk," he could use the words "run" or "stroll"; but this word begins with a "w," so he can make a reasonable guess at the proper word, "walk." This use of contextual clues usually results in a better performance in reading then in spelling as time goes by.

The best way to analyze handwriting is to have the child write spontaneously to dictation. One can then see the slow, halting, laborious efforts typical of these children. The best way to analyze the arithmetic difficulties is to present the child with a page of different kinds of computation to see how he performs adding, subtracting, carrying, and borrowing, and multiplication and division when appropriate for his age and grade. The person who judges the child's performance in these areas must obviously have a good background in standard school curriculum and know what is appropriate for each age and grade.

It is important that the parent and teacher understand the learning disabled child's unique combination of perceptual weaknesses sufficiently to predict which tasks will give the child difficulty and which will not. For example, if the child has no handwriting problems but has considerable difficulty spelling, he still will have problems copying words from a page since speed in copying is facilitated by ease in spelling. Otherwise, material has to be copied letter by letter rather than by words or phrase units. If the child has very poor handwriting and you are tempted to teach him to type, you must remember that being able to spell and read quickly is a necessary part of rapid typing.

There are several other kinds of impaired functioning related to the learning disabilities already described. Often these children are slow to learn to tell time. Sometimes they have trouble memorizing sequences like days of the week or months of the year.

Following verbal directions may be hard for some children because they can't retain bits of information in sequence. *Some* of these children are generally low in all verbal ability while strong in nonverbal intelligence, such as the analysis of mechanical and structural problems. Such children communicate best in nonverbal ways and may always have difficulty with verbally mediated activities. Many learning disabled children have serious problems learning grammar. Learning foreign languages may be particularly difficult. Again we must stress that disabilities vary greatly from child to child and that these particular difficulties are problems only for some learning disabled children.

The younger child usually has difficulty copying from the board, probably because this task requires keeping one's place by quickly reading phrase units and retaining them until the next glance from one's paper back to the board. Later, after these children have mastered some basic reading skills, they may have great difficulty scanning written material for specific answers to questions. For such children, preparation for completing work sheets or taking tests is best accomplished by having someone else read the subject material aloud. (We will say more about this later as part of our general recommendations.) Sometimes as these children get older they can obtain information from reading silently but quickly lose meaning when they have to read aloud. Still others can express themselves verbally quite well but are unable to complete thoughts when they have to write the material.

Many children with learning disabilities have emotional or behavioral problems of the kind seen in HA children. It is this association of behavior problems with learning disability that is responsible for much of the misinformation about learning disability. Most children with learning disability are easily distracted and have a great deal of difficulty concentrating, particularly on schoolwork. Often they have difficulty sustaining effort not only in their schoolwork, but also in chores around the home and even with projects that are fun for them. These observations have led many to assume that the child is not learning because he is insufficiently motivated or because he is lazy. However, if we take a closer look at the behaviors seen in many learning disabled children, we see that they fit into a pattern typical of the HA child. This cluster of behavioral problems, it will be recalled, includes excessively restless and fidgety behavior, a short attention span, greater emotional lability than in the average child of the same age, much greater difficulty learning from discipline as compared to other children of that age, and social problems that usually involve excessive bossiness and poor social perceptiveness. In addition, the child is often excessively impulsive, that is, he acts without regard to the behavioral consequences. All these behaviors are typical of normal children at a younger age.

Children with this pattern of behavioral immaturity have difficulty in school as a direct result of this problem. Classroom work is more difficult for the child who is easily distracted, has difficulty concentrating, and is impulsive. All HA children tend to underachieve in school. However, the degree of underachievement produced by these HA behavioral problems alone is usually small in comparison to that produced by the kind of perceptual problems involved in learning disabilities. Although some children with learning disabilities have very few of the HA behavioral problems, most of these children do have many of them.

Learning disability and the HA child syndrome are both developmental problems. Developmental problems often come in clusters, and two or three developmental problems may be seen together in the same child. When learning disability is accompanied by HA behavioral problems, we think that it is likely that both sets of problems have been caused by an overall disturbance in biological development.

It is also important to realize that there are some emotional problems that seem to be caused by the learning disability itself. For example, almost all these children sooner or later begin to think of themselves as dumb. If they are basically self-conscious and inner-directed, they may become somewhat depressed or self-depreciating. If they are basically outgoing and other-directed, they are more likely to react by clowning or showing off. It is also quite common for learning disabled children to become stubbornly negative or highly anxious about doing any work in their area of difficulty, as a response to their repeated failures. These emotional problems are different from those associated with the HA child. They seem to be clearly related to the way the world often treats learning disabled children, and many of them could probably be prevented or reduced if we changed our way of handling the children. (We shall comment further on this later.) In contrast, the emotional characteristics associated with the HA child are more basically biological in their origin, and therefore are both less subject to preventive psychological and educational measures and more amenable to biological treatment such as medication.

What happens to children with learning disabilities as they grow older? Do they gradually outgrow their problems? Do they eventually learn to read, spell, and do arithmetic normally? The answer is that these children do improve gradually as they get older, just as normal children improve in their ability to do school-related work as they get older, but that most children with learning disabilities develop more slowly than normal children in the skills that are affected by their problems. For example, if their main problem is with spelling, they improve in their spelling skills but not as much as normal children improve during the same period. In a two-year period we may see that a learning disabled child's spelling has reached a level one and a half years higher than before, but at the same time the normal child's spelling has progressed two years beyond what it was originally. It is important for parents and teachers to recognize, therefore, that the gap between the learning disabled child's performance and that of the normal child gets a little larger as time goes by—*even with special educational measures*. That is, even though the learning disabled child does make progress, he falls *further behind* in the affected subjects as he grows older. This comparative lack of progress can be discouraging, but studies in recent years continue to document this as the usual course. A realistic approach to the problem requires awareness of this probable developmental sequence. Parents and teachers often do not notice this pattern because they are watching only the progress of the learning disabled child and are not comparing it to the progress made by the other children. The child's comparative disadvantages in the areas where he has learning disabilities, however, do not mean that he cannot master other kinds of material. We shall return to this point later.

There are some children who start out in kindergarten or first grade with problems similar to those of learning disabled children, but then gain fairly rapidly in development at around the age of eight and seem to catch up in these skills. These children are often referred to as "late bloomers." However, it would be a mistake for parents to pin their hopes on the possibility that their child might belong to this late blooming group. Not many children fall into that category, and those that do usually have somewhat milder problems to begin with.

Although most learning disabled children eventually do learn to read and write and compute well enough to meet the requirements of their average daily tasks, it is also typical for learning problems to persist into adulthood. Most adults who had learning disabilities when they were younger still find themselves unable to spell or read as well as the average adult.

It is also important to note that both normal children and learning disabled children undergo leaps and starts and then plateaus of development all the way through elementary school. Brain development seems to follow the same general pattern as that seen in physical growth. We all know that children may leap forward in height and weight and then stay at that level for several months before making another leap in these measurements. Likewise, a child may be unable to learn a particular concept over a period of three or four months and then suddenly be able to grasp it in a very short period of time. These normal jumps and lags in development should not be confused with the progress that might be made as the result of special education treatment. If, for example, the child was making one of these leaps forward in development at the same time that he was placed in a special education class, the parent or the teacher might mistakenly assume that the progress was due to the special education placement rather than to a normal spurt in development.

As we said at the beginning of this chapter, little is known about the underlying cause of learning disability. We have described learning disability as a developmental problem, but little is known about the nature of that problem. Since the brain is responsible for normal development, we assume that in some respect the brain is functioning inadequately when intellectual development does not proceed at the normal pace. Although we do not know what kind of problem might be involved, we do know that there is no evidence of brain damage in learning disabled children. Some people refer to "wires being hooked up wrong" or to deficiencies in certain chemicals, but there is no firm evidence for either of these possibilities. We do know also that learning disorders have a strong inherited component. When we see learning disability in a child, we usually find that some fairly close family relative had similar difficulties.

There also seems to be a slight relationship between learning disability and the kinds of problems in pregnancy and childbirth that might be expected to affect brain development. However, most children who came from difficult pregnancies or deliveries are normal and show no evidence of learning disturbance. We think that problems such as prematurity or anoxia at birth generally do not produce learning disabilities, but that they *may* contribute to the development of learning disabilities in the susceptible child. Sometimes, for example, in a family with several children, all the children seem to learn normally except one, and that child's prenatal history or his birth was attended by some problem that might have affected brain development. If one takes a closer look at the family, one sees evidence of minor problems in learning in other family members. It is possible that an inherited tendency became a full-blown learning disability problem only in the child whose birth was accompanied by problems.

Recommendations

What to do about reading and spelling difficulties is, of course, a serious practical problem. Children with these difficulties constitute a perplexing problem for educators as well as parents, for there are many theories as to how such children should be taught, and so far no single form of remedial education has been shown to be better than other forms.

The initial questions about how to obtain help arise when the parents first begin to suspect that their child has learning difficulties. Usually the parents' suspicions have been aroused because their child's academic performance does not seem in keeping with his intelligence. In many schools, special educators are available for consultation, and they can perform the necessary intelligence and achievement testing in order to determine if a child is having specific difficulties in reading, spelling, or math. (See the final chapter for additional suggestions regarding special education consultation.)

Once the degree of the child's difficulties has been assayed, it is necessary to try to determine whether some factor other than perceptual deficits is contributing to the problems. As we have indicated, hyperactivity and learning disabilities often occur together, and unfortunately the school consultation staff is not always able to determine whether the child is having HA problems as well. Furthermore, some diagnosticians still regard children of average intelligence with academic performance problems as having such difficulties because of "emotional problems." As we also indicated earlier, the belief that emotional problems are the only cause of a child's academic problems is very seldom supported by the evidence. It is far more likely that inborn perceptual or temperamental handicaps (or both) are producing the learning disabilities—and that these in turn are causing the emotional problems that the educator sees in the school context. Characteristically, in such instances, the child often has few "emotional problems" when he is out of school, but feels worried, anxious, and fearful in school. He feels as we would if entered without preparation in a class in Intermediate Chinese and told that we would not get our weekly paychecks unless we got good grades.

Thus, in approaching the problem of what to do about learning disabilities, it is important to find out first whether hyperactivity is playing a role. If the child with academic problems is also having behavioral problems, either at home or at school, the parents should obtain a consultation with a child psychiatrist. Because child psychiatrists differ in their ideas about how to treat hyperactivity, parents should discuss with their physician not only the possibility that the child may be hyperactive, but also the possibility that medication may be a useful adjunct in the treatment of the child by increasing his attention span and increasing his frustration tolerance. We will amplify this point in the final chapter.

If medication does not make a significant change in the child's learning difficulties, or if the child does not seem to have the kind of problems for which medication is commonly prescribed, questions then arise about which special education procedures should be adopted. For example, parents frequently ask whether the learning disabled child should be placed in a special class or remain in his regular class with additional help from the school's "resource room." Our feeling is that if the child is of average or greater-than-average intelligence and has no problems in understanding and participating in class discussions or in understanding material that the teacher and the other children read aloud, he should remain in his regular classroom. On the other hand, if the child's general learning ability is below average or if his learning problems are so severe that he cannot keep up with material read out loud or discussed, he should probably be placed in a special class.

If the school has a resource room, often the learning disabled child will spend a small portion of each day there. In the resource room the children are usually taught individually or in groups of three or four by a teacher trained in special education. The theory is that the child works in the resource room on the subject that gives him the greatest difficulty, such as reading or spelling, while remaining in his regular class for most other work. In this way he presumably retains an image of himself as a "normal" child.

The resource teacher uses special materials and techniques in working with the learning disabled child. For example, usually a child without learning difficulties is taught the letters through a process of copying what he sees printed in books, on work sheets, or on the board. For most children, copying is all that is required to learn to write letters. For the learning disabled child who has difficulty acquiring this skill, additional procedures may be introduced. He may be taught to trace letters with his finger, which helps develop the muscular sense of how letters are formed, a process called "proprioception." He may also be taught to feel large letter shapes with his eyes closed, which develops his sense of how the letters feel—the kinesthetic sense. Educators are now developing a number of such techniques and trying them out with learning disabled children, but as yet there have been very few careful studies on the extent of their effects.

In addition to providing such special techniques, special education to a great extent is simply extra repetition and drill on a more individualized basis. This seems a sensible procedure. If, for example, a child is having trouble learning to catch a ball, it seems reasonable to practice it over and over again. Practice may not make perfect, but it usually makes a skill somewhat better.

A resource room functions best if it frees the child from doing work in the regular class that he cannot handle, while at the same time concentrating on his problems. For example, if the other children are reading aloud from a book at grade level at the same time that the reading disabled child is reading and practicing at his own level in the resource room, he is spared the embarrassment of constantly being compared unfavorably with the other children. In such instances the resource room may be of some value both educationally and in terms of the child's self-esteem.

However, this ideal situation seldom exists. Most resource room programs provide only 30 to 60 minutes of help each day. The child may be scheduled to leave his regular classroom during an activity in which he does well and to return just as the regular class is beginning his worst subject. We know of one child who attributed his reading failure to his predictable removal daily from the regular class reading session, which thus was never adequately explained to him.

Further, many resource programs focus on reading and spelling and exclude math. Special techniques may sometimes be useful in teaching children with arithmetic difficulties (for example, emphasizing the position of columns, separating up from down), but frequently these are not used. Sometimes learning disabled children with arithmetic difficulties are mistakenly—and uselessly— placed in special reading classes.

Thus, it is possible that the value of the resource room approach has been overestimated. Very little research has been done, and that which has been completed suggests a pessimistic conclusion. The resource room was developed on the theory that children with milder degrees of learning disability could reach normal levels of achievement with a minimal amount of special education intervention. The available data do not, by and large, support this idea. Another reason for the resource room approach is to promote the educational idea of "mainstreaming," which means keeping the child in as normal an environment as possible. It is our impression, however, that the resource room sometimes acquires much the same stigma as a special class.

Because of the problems associated with such stigmatizing, and because so little time is usually available in the resource room program, many parents seriously consider out-of-school individual tutoring. For many of these children individual tutoring may be helpful. In the first place, if the tutor is sensitive, warm, and accepting, the learning disabled child may be able to establish a very therapeutic relationship, which can help to overcome some of the self-esteem problems from which these children frequently suffer. Second, the tutor can try a variety of special education techniques, and can work more intensively with the child on each of them over a longer period of time. In this way, the tutor can judge which techniques seem to be most helpful to the child. The tutor is also in a position to judge whether, as sometimes happens, the special techniques and the intensive work are not significantly altering the child's rate of achievement. (We will say more about this situation below.) Still another advantage of the tutor is the provision of continuity over the entire year; this is particularly important for these children because they often have difficulty in retaining material as well as difficulty in learning it, and tend to forget a great deal during summer vacation. Summer tutoring can minimize the loss of material learned during the previous school year. Finally, the tutor is able to supply remedial help without the emotional tension that sometimes accompanies remedial help that the parents attempt to supply themselves. We should add one word of caution about tutoring, and that is that sometimes the tutor's personality and the child's personality do not "fit," and the parents may prematurely conclude that the tutoring is not successful. It is certainly worth trying another tutor if the first one does not seem to be working well with the child. Further, under any circumstances, a trial of a year or so may be necessary before one can adequately judge whether the tutoring is worthwhile.

For some learning disabled children there seem to be limits to the amount of progress that can be anticipated, regardless of the amount of time and attention that is given to reading, writing, and spelling. To illustrate by analogy, someone with good physical coordination can learn to perform a physical feat by watching someone perform it once or twice. Someone with average coordination may have to practice five or ten times in order to perform the same feat. A person with very poor physical coordination makes no such progress, and endless practice seems to result in very tiny degrees of improvement. Thus, while the resource room and special tutoring may be useful to some children, we urge parents, teachers, and tutors to watch out for the child who becomes increasingly anxious when protracted attempts at remedial education do not produce significant results. This is often a sign to "back off" and to allow the child to move in other directions. As we have said, learning disabled children are frequently talented and imaginative in other areas, and it is better that they achieve a sense of mastery in, say, art, auto mechanics, crafts, or music than that they become increasingly frustrated and suffer decreasing self-esteem attempting to master that which they have great difficulty doing.

However, because success with special educational techniques is often minimal even with children who are interested in and show some flair for various academic subjects, we are going to emphasize below a different kind of approach—one that allows the child to make use of his intelligence to learn the subject matter —while avoiding those tools of learning that he has such difficulty mastering.

WORKING AROUND THE LEARNING PROBLEM

For the child with learning disabilities and average or above-average intelligence, an enormous dilemma is posed by the disparity between his intelligence, his learning disabilities, and the level at which teaching usually occurs. If the child can read material only at the second-grade level but can understand material written at the sixth-grade vocabulary level, then his learning of such subjects as social studies, science, history, literature, geography, and sometimes even abstract math is impeded by forcing him to study only that material which he can read. It is because of such dilemmas that some specialists in learning disabilities are increasingly recommending that education by means of the oral mode should be encouraged for the learning disabled child. Although this technique is relatively new, it has been recognized by some school systems, which have incorporated various aspects of it into their special education facilities.

If the family and the child are to learn this new method, they must first recognize clearly the child's areas of difficulty so that they will know what type of work assignment will be affected by the learning disabilities. Second, they must learn how to get around that problem by helping the child to complete much of the work in a different way—the oral way. Take, for example, the problem in reading. If the child is, say, a fifth-grader and reads comfortably only material at the second-grade level, then the family must be able to recognize when his schoolwork demands grade-level reading and the retention of that material. Examples of such work are assigned chapters in textbooks, writing projects that involve answering questions after reading paragraphs containing the relevant information, and story problems in arithmetic. With assignments of this kind it will be necessary to find some way to have the material read to the child. With a younger child, the parents, older siblings, and tutor might take turns doing the reading. With older children, it is helpful to have the longer work assignments—for example, chapters of textbooks—put on audio tape. This will allow the child to review the material just prior to tasks requiring him to answer questions based on it. As we mentioned, some schools already have some records and cassettes of this kind available for use by learning disabled children. If not, cooperative effort by parents, siblings, and tutor to produce recorded assignments is likely to be very helpful to the child. For shorter assignments, any oral help that the family can provide to the child—reading paragraphs, reading story problems—will help him to complete the written questions and problems. In some communities, Talking Books for the Blind can be made available to the learning disabled child if a physician certifies that the child is dyslexic. With all audio materials, it is sometimes helpful if the child tries to read the text while simultaneously listening to the tape or record. The teacher should also be asked both to read the homework assignment and to write it on the blackboard.

An analogous procedure is required in order to help learning disabled children with writing problems. One such problem is the inability to spell. If the child has difficulty with spelling, any writing task will be extremely slow unless someone is available to spell words for him. Many parents and teachers recommend that the child just work with the dictionary, but the kind of severity of spelling that is involved in learning disability makes that solution impossible. On the average, the child must look up three or four words per sentence, and his inability to spell means that he sometimes does not know where in the dictionary to look for the words that he seeks. For those of us with "normal" spelling problems, the dictionary is a useful tool. For the learning disabled child, it may be an impenetrable maze.

The second part of writing problems involves perceptual-motor incoordination, the inability to develop a smoothly coordinated writing process. Sometimes learning disabled children with motoric writing problems benefit by learning to type. Although this is not helpful in daily school situations, it is useful for homework assignments and for daily schoolwork that is finished at home.

Another approach to writing problems is the use of oral examinations to test the child's knowledge of a subject. Oral examinations are commonly used for evaluating graduate students because it is recognized that such examinations provide the most sensitive way of discovering how much the graduate student knows. Oral examinations are particularly useful with the learning disabled child because they bypass difficulties in both spelling and in writing. Certainly oral examinations are more difficult for the teacher and are not traditional in grammar schools, but without them the teacher may greatly underestimate how much the child knows. The function of the schools is to teach children, and the most important part of such teaching is finding out how much the child knows. One of us (EHW) has found this technique very helpful for estimating the child's academic progress. Parent-teacher associations and special education teachers may be able to help parents work out arrangements whereby oral testing is possible.

Compensating techniques such as audio aids and oral examinations are strongly resisted by both parents and teachers because they are concerned that the child will never learn to read and write adequately and to work independently. They tend to forget that for most of us reading and writing are means, not ends. They are ways of acquiring and communicating knowledge, but what is most important is the knowledge itself—not how it is acquired or communicated. We know of several bright learning disabled children who went through college and obtained advanced degrees by learning to incorporate alternate techniques into their daily school life. Some paid friends to read books into tapes for them; some paid for secretarial services to type their dictated papers. We are confident that this kind of independence can be achieved, and that it is more likely to happen if the child feels good about himself, which is the main thrust of these compensating efforts.

SOME CONCLUDING SUGGESTIONS

If the learning disabled child is hyperactive as well and is taking medicine, there is an additional way in which the parents may be of help to him. As they are helping him with his work, they should carefully watch the effects of the medicine. They may be able to observe whether medication simply decreases his immature behavior or whether it makes it easier for him to learn by improving his attention span and his desire to please others, and making him more tolerant of drill and repetition. If the medication does seem to increase the child's potential for learning, the parents and the tutor should see that the child is receiving it at the same time that he is receiving his remedial help.

Most of the recommendations in this chapter have focused on ways to help the child to master his academic schoolwork. Although it is not yet clear which kinds of help are best for which children, many learning disabled children do make sufficient progress, by means of some of these aids, to do good academic work in a variety of areas. But sometimes even with these extra efforts by parents, teachers, tutor, and child, academic work remains very difficult for the child. It is especially important to remember in such instances that children with learning disabilities not only have obvious academic weaknesses but also may have special strengths in nonacademic areas. We cannot emphasize strongly enough the importance of developing the special assets of the learning disabled child, not only to help him realize his full potential but also to help him maintain his self-esteem. It is psychologically imperative that he have the experience of success. This may, with the best of help, never happen in "academic" areas, but if he can derive a sense of self-worth and mastery from achieving in other areas—from horticulture to folk singing, from carpentry to costume design—it may greatly improve his emotional well-being and thus provide the basis for further development.

7

Finding Help

As we have discussed, frequently problems that may be related to hyperactivity or learning disabilities are first recognized in school by teachers, guidance counselors, or psychologists, who may call the parents' attention to these problems. In some instances, the parents themselves begin to suspect that their child has behavior or learning problems that are beyond the normal range. We wish to emphasize again that in either case, in order to ascertain the probable sources of the child's difficulties, the parents *must* consult a physician who is knowledgeable about the entire range of children's physical and emotional problems, including hyperactivity.

If the parents do not already have a physician for the child and are wondering what kind of specialist to look for, they will find that the following kinds of physicians are most likely to be acquainted with the problems of hyperactivity: child psychiatrists—M.D.s who have studied both adult and child psychiatry; child neurologists—M.D.s who have specialized in disorders of the nervous system in both adults and children; pediatricians—M.D.s who have specialized in diseases of children. As previously indicated, psychologists, who are not physicians, tend to be less familiar with the problems and cannot prescribe medication. The same comment holds true for social workers and school guidance counselors: they are helpful in dealing with any associated family problems that may be present but they cannot offer medication, the most useful and, as repeatedly said, sometimes the only treatment needed.

If the child's pediatrician is consulted, the parents should be aware that some pediatricians have little training in dealing with behavior problems. Parents should frankly ask the pediatrician if he or she does have familiarity with behavior problems, and if not, parents should ask for a recommendation to someone who might be more experienced in this field.

There is no foolproof way of finding a good physician, but there are some helpful procedures that can be followed. If the parents live near a university medical school, they might first inquire if any of the *senior* staff see private patients. Physicians associated with medical schools are not necessarily better trained than physicians in the community. There are excellent, good, fair, poor, and incompetent doctors in both settings. The *probability* is greater, however, that a doctor chosen at random is well trained if he is associated with a medical school. Parents should first request that the child be seen by a child psychiatrist or child neurologist, or if these kinds of physicians are not available, by a psychiatrist who is familiar with the problems of children. If the physicians at the medical school do not see private patients, parents can inquire as to which physicians in the community had been chief residents in child psychiatry, psychiatry, or child neurology in years past. The chief resident is the trainee who, in general, has risen to the top of his group and has been considered qualified to assume, in effect, a junior staff position as chief of the other trainees.

If there is no university medical school available, parents should attempt to locate a directory of medical specialists that lists by state and city the kinds of physicians indicated above. Specialized diplomas and jobs, of course, do not guarantee excellence, but specialized training and experience in these areas increase the likelihood that the physician will be familiar with HA and its treatment.

There are a number of things that parents can do to help the physician evaluate the child. The first is to obtain a written report from the school describing the child's behavior, his academic performance, and any psychological tests that may have been given. The next is to think about what the child's problems have been as he has developed from one stage to another, how they may have been associated with problems within the family, and what events or attitudes seem to have made them better or worse. Gathering information in this way will facilitate the physician's task.

After having discussed the problem with the physician, parents should feel free to inquire how much the consultations will cost and how many visits will be necessary.

Parents should also inquire whether the physician uses medication in the treatment of children. This last question is necessary because not all child psychiatrists do use medication. Some avoid medication as a matter of principle because they believe all behavior problems have psychological causation. Others, mainly adult psychiatrists, have not had experience in treating children with medication.

Inquiring of the physician *how* he or she treats children is sometimes difficult. Physicians tend (quite appropriately) to be somewhat suspicious about patients who question their manner of treatment, and for a number of reasons. First, most physicians are beleaguered by patients who have read glowing reports of "Wondercillin" in popular magazines and come in requesting treatment that has often been underevaluated or overdramatized. Second, most physicians, understandably, do not feel that the patient should recommend the treatment. No physician in his right mind would remove a gallbladder simply because a patient requested it. This medical attitude carries over into psychiatry, even though it is the least scientific of the medical specialties and there is still considerable debate as to what treatment is best for what disorders. Finally, and perhaps most important of all, physicians have learned to be leery of patients who are "shopping around" for treatment. Physicians have learned from experience that many patients do not want to know the truth or the correct treatment and may try doctor after doctor until they find one who tells them what they want to hear. This happens in psychiatry and perhaps somewhat more often in child psychiatry. Some parents may want the doctor to tell them that the problem is the child's problem. The parents may be unwilling to acknowledge that the problem is in the relationship between themselves or between one of them and their child. Such parents will search for a physician who agrees that the problem is totally within the child. Accordingly, many physicians have learned to suspect the parent who wants treatment only for the child. But the point here is that although almost all HA children can benefit if the parents become aware of their own personal problems, this is not sufficient treatment for the HA child. The parents must make certain that the physician is willing to examine problems that are within the child, that is, constitutional problems, as well as those between the child and the parents.

The parents must therefore in this case act in a way that is not customary in choosing a physician. In medicine most well-trained physicians are in quite close agreement on how to treat most disorders. In psychiatry, since there is much less agreement and very little *evidence* concerning the effectiveness of various forms of treatment, any physician who claims certainty should be somewhat suspect. Some psychiatrists prefer medication, some individual psychotherapy, some group psychotherapy, some various combinations of these. There are many psychiatrists who are flexible and use different approaches with different patients or multiple approaches with the same patient. There are other psychiatrists who limit themselves to one approach or one sort of patient. Obviously the parents want a physician who is not committed to only one approach. If the physician only gives medicine or never uses medicine, he or she is not the physician to choose. Thus, the parents should feel free to ask if the physician uses medicine in the treatment of children. If opposed *in principle,* the physician is not an open-minded student of child psychiatry. If the physician rarely uses medicine, or feels that it is rarely needed, he or she is probably committed to a school of thought that attributes most behavioral problems to psychological causes, and should not treat a hyperactive child. This kind of doctor would undoubtedly disagree vehemently with us and claim that we are misled. We would argue that that physician has had relatively little experience in the use of medication in hyperactive children and is therefore not in an adequate position to judge its usefulness.

In any event the parents should remember certain principles that apply to *any* consultation with a physician. First, it is proper to inquire how long the treatment will last and how much the treatment will cost. Second, it is always proper to request another consultation or evaluation. Third, if the treatment prescribed (medical or psychological) is not working at all after a reasonable period of time, say six months, another consultation *should* be requested. Fourth, it must be remembered that all problems are not solvable in all people, adults or children. Psychological techniques do not work in all people whose problems are psychological in origin, and medical treatments do not work in all people whose problems are physical in origin. However, parents should follow one of the oldest medical principles: if what is being done works, stick with it! If what is being done is not working, consider trying something else!

Finding Help for the Learning Disabled Child

Finding help for the child who is learning disabled as well as hyperactive, or who has learning disabilities without hyperactivity, may pose some special problems. Although physicians can help the HA child, they are not in a position to provide educational help for problems stemming from learning disabilities. Accordingly, the hyperactive, learning disabled child whose HA is being treated, or the learning disabled but not hyperactive child, requires additional educational help.

As we said previously, many school systems have special educators who can administer the tests necessary to diagnose the existence of learning disability and to pinpoint specific problem areas. If the school system does not have a special education staff, help can be obtained in *some* communities from special educators in private practice. If neither school nor private special educators are available, other possible sources of help are local teachers' colleges or university departments of education with programs in special education. The directors of these special education programs should be able to help parents find someone competent to *test* the learning disabled child. Once the child has been tested and his difficulties assayed, the diagnostician— whether in school, in private practice, or in a graduate department of special education—will work with the parents and the child, recommending various combinations of schoolwork and tutoring to see what works best in terms of the child's particular difficulties and assets, and also in terms of what is available at the child's school. The diagnostician should be able to help the parents to find the necessary tutors.

The Association for Children with Learning Disabilities can often be helpful in locating diagnostic and therapeutic help. The association is a nonprofit organization composed of parents and interested professionals whose aim is to increase the recognition of hyperactivity and learning disabilities and to foster improved care for children with such problems. If there is a chapter of the ACLD in the community, parents should get in touch with it. Not only does this organization almost always have information concerning community resources, but also its meetings provide parents with the invaluable moral support that comes from realizing that many people are facing and working on the same problems. To find out the location of the nearest chapter of the ACLD, write to the national office: Association for Children with Learning Disabilities, 4156 Library Road, Pittsburgh, Pennsylvania 15234.

In all areas of life there may be no perfect solutions to significant problems, but there are always better approaches and worse ones. It has been the aim of this book to point toward better approaches that are now available in the treatment of the hyperactive child and the learning disabled child.

Index

135